Total Bliss

DISCOVER TRUE JOY
IN PHILIPPIANS

Linda Barrick

Published by Hope Out Loud © 2015 Linda Barrick

ISBN 978-0-9968063-0-5

To order additional copies of this resource: Write Hope Out Loud, PO Box 2366, Forest, VA 24551; email Andy@hopeoutloud.com; order on-line at www.hopeoutloud.com.

Project supervision by Christy Murphy

Editing by Janet Martin

Graphic Design by Marnie Whitten

Portraits by Cassie Foster

Printed in the United States of America

Hope Out Loud
PO Box 2366, Forest, VA 24551

CONTENTS

MEET THE AUTHOR

Linda Barrick, author of *Miracle for Jen*, is an inspirational speaker with a captivating message of hope. A graduate of Liberty University, Linda leads a weekly Bible study of over 500 women at Thomas Road Baptist Church in Lynchburg, Va, where she lives with her husband Andy of 26 years and their two children Jennifer and Joshua.

Their lives were dramatically changed 9 years ago when a drunk driver struck their family van head on going 80 miles an hour. Jennifer suffered a traumatic brain injury and was not expected to live through the night. But God miraculously intervened. Now at age 24, God has given Jennifer a new personality and a new platform to share Christ.

God is using the entire Barrick family in ways they never dreamed possible. They travel all over the country speaking at teen and women's events, schools, disability centers, churches and community events. God is using their story to change thousands of lives with a message of faith, hope and forgiveness.

The Barrick Family has a daily international radio program and a ministry called *Hope Out Loud* that provides encouragement to hurting people and families all over the world. Linda has been interviewed on numerous radio and television programs including *Fox and Friends, NBC Today Show, CBN* and *Life Today*.

Linda's greatest joy is being a wife and a mom. She has learned to treasure every day as a precious gift from God. She loves going to her son's baseball games, spending time with friends, going on adventures with her husband and drinking coffee with whipped cream on top. For over 24 years, Linda has enjoyed leading prayer groups and Bible studies. Talking to women, hearing their stories and discipling them to fall more in love with Jesus is her passion.

Connect with Linda at **linda@Hopeoutloud.com.**

INTRODUCTION

I had barely turned twenty when I married Andy, my high school sweetheart. We fell in love when I was still in braces and he didn't have a single hair on his chest. We were young and immature, but I was certain that he was the man of my dreams. Last year, we celebrated a quarter of a century! Andy ran around announcing, "We've been married for 25 years, and it's been nothing but total *bliss* … (followed by a roar of hysterical laughter)." It became our running household joke. Anyone who has been married for more than 24 hours knows that marriage is not always "total bliss."

Even though I married God's choice for my life and I could never survive without him, we've had our share of ups and downs. We've had wins and losses, made money and lost money, built roots and ripped them up relocating. We've changed careers, had miscarriages, been threatened with lawsuits, betrayed by friends, suffered chronic pain from injuries—you know, all the regular stuff that is just a hazardous byproduct of living.

Through the years, Philippians has become our "go-to" book. It's the place we go to find strength and joy. No other book of the Bible packs so much wisdom and hope in four short chapters. But what I love the most about Philippians is that the words are not merely empty, sugarcoated promises. They come straight from the heart of God through an author who understood intense pain and disappointment. Paul writes this book while he is in prison in a foreign country, suffering from a severe physical affliction, waiting to find out if he gets to live or die! If this guy could find joy in those circumstances, I want what he's got!

Philippians is full of buried treasure—secrets that God has preserved for us throughout centuries of human suffering. They are meant for us to discover and put into practice. We will dig into the background information on the book of Philippians and people of Philippi, then break Philippians down into four lessons that coincide with the four chapters to uncover Paul's secret to joyful living:

Acts 16:6-40 - Joy Behind the Scenes (week 1)
Philippians 1 - Joy in Suffering (week 2)
Philippians 2 - Joy in Serving (week 3)
Philippians 3 - Joy in Believing (week 4)
Philippians 4 - Joy in Giving (week 5)

I don't know your story, but I do know life is rarely "nothing but total bliss." As I'm writing this Bible study, we have a 24-year-old daughter with a traumatic brain injury who recently had thyroid cancer surgery. My husband finished treatments for prostate cancer this summer (twenty years before you are supposed to get it). And the last time we were at the brain doctor, he recommended that I do some therapy sessions because my memory was showing signs of dysfunction (or maybe I'm just 47 and leaking hormones)! Some days life feels so impossible and I think if I start crying, I may never stop!

No, "total bliss" does not describe my circumstances, and I'm guessing it doesn't describe yours either. **But I do know this…there is a Source of JOY inside me that is always available when I reach for it. My heart, mind and soul can literally tap into a reservoir of "total bliss" at any given time and the words in Philippians help me get there!** I want you to be able to find that joy too. My prayer is that through this study of Philippians you will not only fall in love with God's Word, but you will get to know the Source of those words and the Source of your joy no matter what you are facing today.

"And this is my prayer: that your love may abound more and more in knowledge and depth of insight, so that you may be able to discern what is best and may be pure and blameless for the day of Christ, filled with the fruit of righteousness that comes through Jesus Christ—to the glory and praise of God" (Philippians 1:9-11).

Let's Go For It – "Nothing but Total Bliss!"

Linda Barrick

My daughter Jen still struggles with her short-term memory every day, but she is an instrument of hope that God speaks through. She often doesn't remember to be worried or feel loss; she unequivocally trusts her Heavenly Father and speaks His promises out loud over every problem. Jen replaces her problems with the sound of His promises. I will be weaving her prayers throughout this study to encourage you and give you hope to try it too!

PRAYER FROM JEN

When I Need Joy!

Dear Faithful Father,

As I am sitting here, the sun is so beautiful. I love how it warms my soul and fills me up with You. Also, the birds…WOW…they are always praising You and happy as ever! Lord, help me to have that kind of happiness and to be praising You no matter what the circumstances. Please Lord, fill me up today with everything that You are. Draw me close to You and never let me go. Thank you for the JOY You have been giving me– it is overflowing! Amen.

Following after You with my whole heart!

"But let all who take refuge in you be glad; let them ever sing for joy. Spread your protection over them, that those who love your name may rejoice in you."
Psalm 5:11

A NOTE TO LEADERS

I am praying for you as you invite women to journey along with you through Philippians. When I moved to Virginia, a friend asked me if I would start a Bible study in my home. I said yes thinking only three people would come. Before I knew it, there were neighbors, friends, and people I had never met packed into my little family room, sitting on the floor and everywhere. Not to mention tons of kids, toys, and noise with a babysitter in the basement. I felt very inadequate. **But God whispered to my heart, "It's not about your Bible knowledge, or how clean your house is or the size of your home. It's about women feeling loved, accepted and knowing you care."** The most important thing was that the presence of God was there and women felt the love of Jesus the moment they walked through the door.

Whether you meet in your home, at work, or at church, pray before your small group begins and invite God's presence to be with you. Pray that each lady would feel loved and accepted the moment they walk in your front door or pull their chair up to your table. Even if you are in a big room at church, picture that the ladies God has given you to serve just walked into your home.

BEFORE YOU GET STARTED

The Scriptures included in the following pages are from the New International Version (NIV) to make it easy for you to answer the questions and participate in this study wherever you go (school parking lot, waiting rooms, baseball games, your office, etc.). However, nothing is more exciting than opening your Bible to highlight, underline and circle the things God teaches you. I encourage you to read Philippians in a couple different Bible translations, so you have a richer understanding of what Paul is saying.

God's Word is alive and powerful. Before you open God's Word, pray first and ask the Holy Spirit (God Himself who lives inside of you) to teach you and help you understand what you are reading. The Holy Spirit can help the Bible come to life for you and give you insight like you have never known. The questions are designed to lead you back to specific verses to give the Holy Spirit a chance to speak directly to you. **You don't have to worry about having the "right" answers; just give God a chance to reveal Himself to you.**

I wish you could see my Bible. It might look worn and tattered to some, but it is a treasure to me. The margins are filled with the things God has whispered to my heart. It is something that I plan to pass on to my children as a legacy of God's faithfulness. As God speaks to you, write down what He says in the margin of your Bible or this study guide. Like Paul, you too can leave written evidence that God was alive and active in your life.

There are five weeks of homework in this Bible study and a video to watch at the beginning of each week. You can go at your own pace…starting and stopping where you need to since there are no specific divisions for each day.

Action Steps are woven throughout to help you apply the truths of Philippians to your everyday life.

Journal Response is at the end of each week for you to write out your prayers and thoughts to God. He longs to have a personal, intimate love relationship with you. Prayer is simply talking to the One who loved you before you were even born. God created you and He takes great delight in you! As God speaks to your heart, this is a page for you to respond back to Him.

I'm asking God to change all of our lives forever through the pages of Philippians.

I believe that is about to happen!
Let's get started…

Joy Behind the Scenes

WEEK 1 VIDEO NOTES

Happiness depends on outward circumstances.

Joy depends on our relationship with Jesus.

Chara = Greek word for joy which means "to be exceedingly glad"

No one can take away your_____!

It is a _____from God.

Rejoice when you face trials of many kinds (James 1:2-4)!

- Test my faith

- Develop _____

- Make me mature and _____

God can use us WHERE we are and AS we are!

When Paul wrote Philippians, he was:

- In prison

- Waiting to find out if he will live or die

- Suffering from a _____ (2 Corinthians 12:7-9)

Acts 16:6-10
- Paul and his companions are being led by the _____.
- First time the Gospel is shared in Europe!

Acts 16:11-34
Church at Philippi is started with 3 unlikely people:

- _____

- Slave Girl

- _____

Joy Behind the Scenes

A few years ago, my father pulled our immediate family together and announced that he needed to have emergency open-heart, quadruple by-pass surgery. While the doctors had given us every indication that the surgery would be successful, it was still a very somber moment because we all knew that my grandfather (my dad's dad) had passed away in the middle of this same surgery. Even though many medical improvements had been made since the past generation, it didn't change the fact that the next morning they were going to cut his chest cavity in half, stop his heart, do surgery and then hope his heart responded when it was time to start pumping on its own.

God, in his mercy, had given my mother unexplainable peace that dad was going to survive. But, each of us still had to face the unavoidable yet unspoken question: What if dad doesn't make it? We spent the evening praying, crying, hugging, telling old stories, laughing and praying some more. At the end of our family time, my dad disappeared and came back with four handwritten letters—one for my mother and one for each of us three children. Evidently, he had faced the same question.

I remember him saying: "I hope you aren't going to need these. I plan to be around for a lot longer to tell you in person how much I love you. Just in case, I wanted you to have it in writing from my own hand how much you mean to me and how much joy you have brought me in my lifetime."

We each read our letters with tears streaming down our cheeks, and then we did what only siblings would do…we exchanged letters to compare what he had said to each of us. Dad, who knows us better than we know ourselves, knew exactly what words each one of us needed to hear.

My dad has always been my number one encourager. I've always believed I could do anything because he believed in me. I guess I shouldn't have been surprised that at the one moment in life when he could have been panicking or self-absorbed with his own fears, he was thinking about encouraging us.

That's exactly what is happening in the book of Philippians. Paul is stuck in a Roman prison waiting for a death sentence, but he is not one bit worried about himself. He is rejoicing and confident of his future. His only worry is for the fragile faith of the young church in Philippi.

He doesn't want them to lose their hope in God because of his absence and suffering. They feared Paul's prison sentence was ending his ministry, but Paul believed his prison sentence was expanding his ministry. So, in the midst of his life-or-death crisis, he writes an intimate letter to remind his children in the faith how much he loves them. His primary objective is to encourage the believers in Philippi to REJOICE with him because he was certain that God had a higher purpose for his pain:

"Therefore, my dear friends, as you have always obeyed—not only in my presence, but now much more in my absence… [13] for it is God who works in you to will and to act in order to fulfill his good purpose…Then you will shine among them like stars in the sky [16] as you hold firmly to the word of life… [17] But even if I am being poured out like a drink offering…I am glad and rejoice with all of you. [18] So you too should be glad and rejoice with me" (Philippians 2:12-18).

It's a good thing we had those letters. My dad spent 100 days in ICU. We had many scary moments as we watched his whole body go septic. In the end, God spared his life, like mom was always certain He would. At one point, when dad was waking up, he was desperately mouthing two words. My sister and I were sure he was saying "So happy. So happy." Like he was so happy to be with us! Until my brother said, "He's not saying 'so happy;' he's saying 'so thirsty.' He wants you to get him a drink!" There were many days of uncertainty and confusion when my dad was unconscious. In those moments, we were so grateful to have in writing the truth of what he believed about us.

Think of God's Word that way. It's the truth of what your Father believes about you. And on the days when life is scary or hard or uncertain, you have in writing exactly how God feels about you. He knows the exact words you need to hear at just the right time.

Twenty-one of the twenty-seven books in the New Testament are actually letters written to various churches and individuals by the Apostles (eye-witness followers of Jesus) in the first four decades after Jesus rose from the dead and ascended into heaven. They had just seen a dead man walking; so, as you might imagine, they were pretty fired up! Not only that, but they were commissioned with starting the greatest idea in history—the local church.

ACTION STEP
BEFORE YOU EXPLORE THE REST OF THE BACK-STORY, OPEN YOUR OWN BIBLE AND READ PART (OR ALL) OF PHILIPPIANS. ASK GOD TO LEAD YOU TO THE EXACT WORDS YOU NEED TO HEAR TODAY.

Plus, they had just been given the gift of the Holy Spirit, which meant that the Power and Person of God now dwelt inside them and equipped them. Their mission was to go into all the world, preach the gospel, and establish communities of believers who would raise up more followers to do the same (Matthew 28:19-20; Mark 16:15).

At least twelve or thirteen of the New Testament letters were written by the Apostle Paul, the religious zealot and persecutor of Christians turned follower-of-Jesus and church-planter. Philippians was one of his four "prison letters," meaning he wrote this letter while he was in prison. In fact, he wrote it between AD 61 and AD 62 during his first of two prolonged imprisonments in Rome, before being beheaded at the hands of Nero (the evil Emperor of Rome notorious for torturing Christians) five years later in AD 67.

Paul, although under the inspiration of the Holy Spirit, probably never imagined that we would still be reading this letter over 2,000 years later! He wrote it to encourage his fellow believers, but it is still packed with relevant admonition for us. After all, when you are hurting, do you want to take advice from someone who's never had any problems? It's easy to tell people to have joy when life is great, but imagine hearing those words from someone well acquainted with hard times. Imagine this…

> **You are in prison in a foreign country (Philippians 1:12-18).**
>
> **You are suffering from severe physical pain (2 Corinthians 12:7-9).**
>
> **You are waiting to find out if you get to live or die (Philippians 1:20-24).**
>
> **You are separated from the people you love (without cell phone or internet service, Philippians 1:3-8).**

What do you do? You write a letter to encourage other people. And in spite of all of your suffering, you decide to make the theme of your letter *joy*. Eighteen times in just four short chapters, Paul uses the word "joy" or "rejoice." The main idea of Philippians can best be summed up in Philippians 4:4: "Rejoice in the Lord always. I will say it again: Rejoice!"

What in the world has gotten into this guy? Whatever it is, I need some!

It's interesting to note here that the word "gospel" appears nine times in the book of Philippians. It's almost as if we get the picture that our joy doubles in proportion to the gospel. If that is true, then I want the gospel to be at work in my life!

Take a Look

According to 1 Corinthians 15:1-6, what is the "gospel?"

The Bible says that when one person repents and receives the gift of the gospel, it causes the angels to rejoice in heaven (Luke 15). Why does the gospel result in joy?

How can the gospel be at work in our lives on a daily basis? Does it just bring you joy at the point of salvation or can this "good news" offer joy daily?

Let's Get Real

Briefly describe the time when you first believed the gospel for salvation.

Have you ever had the opportunity to share the gospel with someone else who believed it for salvation? How did it make you feel?

Sharing Jesus On the Baseball Field

My son Josh played on a collegiate baseball team this past summer in California. He had the opportunity to travel up and down the coast, go on a missions trip to Mexico, and sit right behind home plate at a Dodgers' baseball game. But the biggest highlight of Josh's summer was working at a Fellowship of Christian Athlete's baseball camp with a group of boys ages 9-10. Someone gave a testimony on the last day of camp and the gospel was presented. One of the boys on Josh's team wanted to know more and didn't fully understand the message of salvation. Josh was able to take him to the side of the baseball field and explain to him how much God loved him and that Jesus died on the cross for him. Immediately, Dillon said, "Yes, I want to ask Jesus into my heart and follow Him." After Josh led him in a salvation prayer, Dillon started jumping up and down, full of excitement! When they walked back to the team and Josh explained what Dillon had done, all the boys started cheering for Dillon. It was a huge celebration because now Dillon was in the family of God. He was a child of the King!

Take a Look: Philippians 1:1-2

Paul's Greeting
¹ Paul and Timothy, servants of Christ Jesus,
To all God's holy people in Christ Jesus at Philippi, together with the overseers and deacons:
² Grace and peace to you from God our Father and the Lord Jesus Christ.

Opening Statement

Traditional letters in our culture begin with "Dear So-and-So" (Recipient) and end with a closure like "Love, (Author's name)." Philippians is exactly opposite. Following the standard ancient Hellenistic format for letter-writing in the first century A.D., Philippians begins with the Author's name, followed by the Recipient's name and a personal greeting. In that sense, it is more like receiving an email where the Author and subject are what you see first in your inbox before you open the contents.

You can tell a lot about a person from the subject of their email. In those first few words they choose, you can tell if they are about to drop a truckload of complaints, thank you, or assign you a task. That opening statement makes a big impression! Likewise, we can learn a lot from Paul's opening statement before we look at the rest of his contents.

 Who is the author of Philippians (verse 1)?

Paul refers to himself and Timothy as "servants of Christ Jesus" (verse 1). The Greek word he uses for "servants" here is doulos, which more specifically describes a slave who had no will or rights or possessions of his/her own. The doulos was to obey his/her master's will immediately and without question.

🐚 *Why do you think Paul chooses this strong servant/slave word to describe himself?*

🐚 *How might his "servant/slave" perspective on life help or hinder him from having joy in adverse circumstances?*

🐚 *Who are the recipients of Paul's letter (verse 1)?*

🐚 *What are the two blessings Paul bestows upon them (verse 2)? What is significant about the order in which those blessings are mentioned?*

🐚 *Here's the important thing…Who or what is the source of those blessings (verse 2)?*

In Latin, Paul's name "Paulus" means "little" or "small," in contrast to his original name "Saul," which no doubt came from King Saul, since they were both from the tribe of Benjamin. Paul refers to himself as the "least of all saints" in Ephesians 3:8.

"Timothy" is a combination of two Greek words meaning "honor" (time) and "God" (theos). He was one who God honored because he honored God. We are not really certain if Timothy was literally with Paul at the time of the writing or helping him pen the letter. We do know that Timothy was with Paul on his second missionary journey when the church of Philippi was birthed (Acts 16:1-3), and Paul wanted to send Timothy to encourage them in his absence (Philippians 1:19-23).

We also know that most of Paul's letters start with the phrase "Paul, an Apostle of Jesus Christ," sort of reaffirming his authority. Only four of his confirmed twelve epistles do not include this formal title. It may be that because Paul had a close, endearing relationship with the church of Philippi, he used a less formal greeting. Or, he may have wanted to establish Timothy's authority since his death was imminent. Either way, Paul deems it unnecessary to assert himself as the only authority of his message. Instead, he opens with a more humble, team approach. Gotta love that guy!

How might the "source" credited in verse 2 help you find joy in the midst of life's sorrow and disappointments?

Let's Get Real

What is one thing you learned about God from Paul's opening statement?

Paul willingly called himself a slave of Jesus Christ. The truth is: We are all slaves to whatever controls us. Being a slave to Christ actually means true freedom. When the King is my Master, I am free from the bondage of sin and strongholds.

 What are some things that could control/enslave you if you aren't careful (for example: food, success, bitterness, busy schedule)?

 If you were writing Philippians in an email to friends, what would your subject line be? Just kidding – made you sweat!

Gospel Ignites in Europe!

Have you ever thought about how churches get started? I live in the South where there is a steeple on almost every corner. Every time I walk into a church, I pretty much take for granted that there will be chairs, pews, bathrooms, children's facilities, etc. Have you ever thought about where it all came from or who started it? My sister and her husband are church planters. They move to new cities and start churches from scratch—no building, no people, no guarantees anyone will even come. I remember my sister asking her husband, "If no one shows up for church, do I have to sit and listen to you preach, or can we just go have breakfast?"

Paul was one of the original church planters. After his conversion, he journeyed from city to city in the Roman Empire preaching and teaching new believers how to assemble together and worship God. Whenever he left one church behind to move on to the next place God was leading him, Paul often wrote letters to encourage them during his absence. Philippians is the letter he wrote to the church of Philippi. **The exciting thing about the church of Philippi is that it was the very first ever-in-the-history-of-the-world church started in Europe!** The Spirit of God miraculously led Paul from modern-day Turkey to modern-day Greece to reach the first Europeans with the gospel of Jesus Christ. You won't believe the amazing events in the backstory on the church of Philippi found in Acts 16:6-40.

Check it out…

ACTION STEP

WRITE A LETTER TO SOMEONE YOU LOVE (YOUR CHILDREN, A PARENT, A SPOUSE, A TEACHER, A FRIEND) LETTING THEM KNOW HOW MUCH YOU LOVE THEM AND ENCOURAGING THEM BY STATING THE POSITIVE THINGS YOU BELIEVE ABOUT THEM.

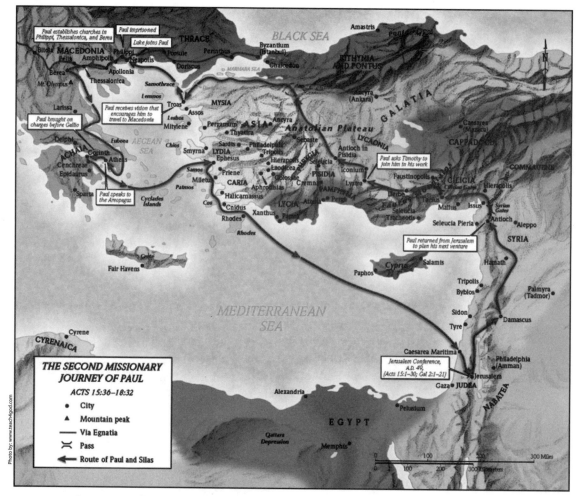

THE SECOND MISSIONARY JOURNEY OF PAUL

ACTS 15:36–18:32

- • City
- ▲ Mountain peak
- — Via Egnatia
- ⤬ Pass
- ◀— Route of Paul and Silas

Take a Look: Acts 16:6-12

Macedonian Call

Paul and his companions traveled throughout the region of Phrygia and Galatia, having been kept by the Holy Spirit from preaching the word in the province of Asia. [7] When they came to the border of Mysia, they tried to enter Bithynia, but the Spirit of Jesus would not allow them to. [8] So they passed by Mysia and went down to Troas. [9] During the night Paul had a vision of a man of Macedonia standing and begging him, "Come over to Macedonia and help us." [10] After Paul had seen the vision, we got ready at once to leave for Macedonia, concluding that God had called us to preach the gospel to them. [11] From Troas we put out to sea and sailed straight for Samothrace, and the next day we went on to Neapolis. [12] From there we traveled to Philippi, a Roman colony and the leading city of that district of Macedonia. And we stayed there several days.

🐚 *Who were Paul's companions mentioned in verse 6?*
(Hint: Acts 15:40, Acts 16:1-5, and the author of Acts who uses the pronoun "we"
several times in the story)

🐚 *Who was leading and directing Paul (verses*
6-10)? Underline the name "God," the
name "Jesus," and the name "Holy Spirit" in
these verses.

NOTE ON THE PRESENCE OF THE TRINITY

This is the only time in the New Testament that all three Persons of the Godhead are present in the calling of a believer to a place of service. At the baptism of Jesus, all three members of the Trinity were present authenticating the beginning of Jesus' ministry. **Amazingly, all three members of the Trinity (God the Father, God the Son Jesus, and God the Holy Spirit) participate in the calling of Paul and his companions to Macedonia as well, which shows how important it was on God's calendar.** It may be because it was the beginning of the gospel being preached in Europe and eventually the Americas. If you are a Gentile Christian from Europe or North or South America, this is the beginning of your spiritual heritage on the pages of Scripture. The entire Trinity was present for it and unified in it! The sovereignty of God always trumps the strategy of men. **Chances are, if you are reading these words in English, you were part of the plan in this calling! God had you in mind!**

🐚 *What happened that caused Paul to change*
course and cross over from Asia Minor (Turkey)
to Europe (Greece) in verses 9-10?

🐚 *What can we learn about God from Paul's*
change in plans?

🐚 *When God redirects us, can we expect Him to provide confirmations that we heard Him correctly? Use Paul's story as evidence.*

🐚 *What city did Paul end up going to and what is significant about this city (verse 12)?*

NOTE ON PHILIPPI

Philippi was an ancient city founded by Philip II, King of Macedonia, because of the nearby gold mines in 356 BC. It is historically famous for one particular event. In 42 BC Mark Antony and Octavian defeated Brutus and Cassius, the assassins of Julius Caesar, in a battle at Philippi. Later in 31 BC when Octavian defeated Antony and Cleopatra, he rebuilt the city of Philippi. He placed retired soldiers there to ensure loyalty to Rome and established it as a military outpost. He also gave the new colony the highest privilege obtainable by a Roman provincial municipality—the ius italicum. Colonists could buy, own, or transfer property and maintain the right to civil lawsuits. When Paul arrives in AD 49, it is twenty-one years before the destruction of the temple in Jerusalem and the Roman exile of the Jews (AD 70). At that time, Philippi was a leading urban center located 10 miles north of the seaport Neapolis ("new city") and was mostly inhabited by Greeks and Romans.

The city is described by historians as the "gate between Asia and Europe." Philippi becomes known in church history as the gateway to European Christianity. Philip II established it, Octavian rebuilt it, Rome perfected it, but God had big plans for it!

Let's Get Real

Often we make our plans first and then ask God to bless them. Paul was doing a good thing by sharing the gospel in Turkey, but God had a better and bigger plan for him in Macedonia. I have always been amazed at the example Jesus set for all of us while He was here on this earth. He was the Son of God, yet Jesus still got up early and went alone to a quiet place to pray to His Father and get the plans for the day (Mark 1:35).

Do you consult your calendar or spend time with God first to find out His plans for the day?

Have you ever felt God nudging you to change your plans? How did you know it was God? What confirmations did you receive?

Do you think we can ask God for signs or confirmations? Do you think asking for confirmation from God indicates a lack of faith or a growing relationship with God?

Have you ever experienced a time when God shut the door on an opportunity you planned and opened the door on something He planned? Whose plan was better?

How does knowing that God will do whatever it takes to get you where He wants you to go help with both anxiety and joy?

My Plan vs. God's Plan

I was so excited to finally have a day to relax. My daughter Jen and I were on our way to get a free massage with a gift certificate someone had given us. I'm driving down the expressway, talking on the phone to my mom and suddenly there is smoke everywhere. "I'm on fire! I'm on fire!" I started screaming in the phone as I realized it was coming from my car engine. Immediately, I pulled off to the side of the road. We jumped out of the car and ran far away to the nearest ditch in case the car exploded.

I tried calling my husband but he didn't answer. A man who worked for the city stopped and asked if he could help. Quickly, he looked at my car engine and diagnosed the problem. While we were waiting for the tow truck to arrive, Jen began sharing her story with him. As it turned out, he too had suffered from years of physical pain and could relate to Jen. Then, out of nowhere, with child-like faith, Jen said, "We have a book about my story in the back of our car. Do you want one?" "Sure!" the man replied. Once the tow truck arrived and he knew we were safe, he left with the *Miracle for Jen* book under his arm. I honestly thought we would never hear from him again.

The next day, I received an email from his girlfriend saying that she stayed up all night reading *Miracle for Jen*. She went on to share how it had changed her perspective and she wanted to have a personal relationship with Jesus. What an amazing story of a life that was changed because my car randomly caught on fire at the very moment when that kind gentleman just happened to be driving past us. Talk about a divine appointment!

 At the repair shop, the mechanic was amazed. "The oil filter we replaced for you last week was defective. Usually when this happens, the oil leaks out immediately in the garage and we can fix it. I have never seen this before! You drove around a whole week before the oil leaked out!"

"Many are the plans in a person's heart; but it is the Lord's purpose that prevails" (Proverbs 19:21).

Take a Look: Acts 16:13-40

Three Conversions at Philippi

1. Jewish Businesswoman → 13-15
¹³ On the Sabbath we went outside the city gate to the river, where we expected to find a place of prayer. We sat down and began to speak to the women who had gathered there. ¹⁴ One of those listening was a woman from the city of Thyatira named Lydia, a dealer in purple cloth.

She was a worshiper of God. The Lord opened her heart to respond to Paul's message. ¹⁵ When she and the members of her household were baptized, she invited us to her home. "If you consider me a believer in the Lord," she said, "come and stay at my house." And she persuaded us.

2. Slave Girl → 16-24

¹⁶ Once when we were going to the place of prayer, we were met by a female slave who had a spirit by which she predicted the future. She earned a great deal of money for her owners by fortune-telling. ¹⁷ She followed Paul and the rest of us, shouting, "These men are servants of the Most High God, who are telling you the way to be saved." ¹⁸ She kept this up for many days. Finally Paul became so annoyed that he turned around and said to the spirit, "In the name of Jesus Christ I command you to come out of her!" At that moment the spirit left her. ¹⁹ When her owners realized that their hope of making money was gone, they seized Paul and Silas and dragged them into the marketplace to face the authorities. ²⁰ They brought them before the magistrates and said, "These men are Jews, and are throwing our city into an uproar ²¹ by advocating customs unlawful for us Romans to accept or practice." ²² The crowd joined in the attack against Paul and Silas, and the magistrates ordered them to be stripped and beaten with rods. ²³ After they had been severely flogged, they were thrown into prison, and the jailer was commanded to guard them carefully. ²⁴ When he received these orders, he put them in the inner cell and fastened their feet in the stocks.

3. Jailer → 25-40

²⁵ About midnight Paul and Silas were praying and singing hymns to God, and the other prisoners were listening to them. ²⁶ Suddenly there was such a violent earthquake that the foundations of the prison were shaken. At once all the prison doors flew open, and everyone's chains came loose. ²⁷ The jailer woke up, and when he saw the prison doors open, he drew his sword and was about to kill himself because he thought the prisoners had escaped. ²⁸ But Paul shouted, "Don't harm yourself! We are all here!" ²⁹ The jailer called for lights, rushed in and fell trembling before Paul and Silas. ³⁰ He then brought them out and asked, "Sirs, what must I do to be saved?" ³¹ They replied, "Believe in the Lord Jesus, and you will be saved—you and your household." ³² Then they spoke the word of the Lord to him and to all the others in his house. ³³ At that hour of the night the jailer took them and washed their wounds; then immediately he and all his household were baptized. ³⁴ The jailer brought them into his house and set a meal before them; he was filled with joy because he had come to believe in God—he and his whole household. ³⁵ When it was daylight, the magistrates sent their officers to the jailer with the order: "Release those men." ³⁶ The jailer told Paul, "The magistrates have ordered that you and Silas be released. Now you can leave. Go in peace." ³⁷ But Paul said to the officers: "They beat us publicly without a trial, even though we are Roman citizens, and threw us into prison. And now do they want to get rid of us quietly? No! Let them come themselves and escort us out." ³⁸ The officers reported this to the magistrates, and when they heard that Paul and Silas were Roman citizens, they were alarmed. ³⁹ They came to appease them and

escorted them from the prison, requesting them to leave the city. [40] After Paul and Silas came out of the prison, they went to Lydia's house, where they met with the brothers and sisters and encouraged them. Then they left.

Despite the fact that Paul had seen a vision of a man from Macedonia begging him to come over and help them, when Paul arrived in Philippi, there were apparently no men worshipping God at the place of prayer. According to Jewish custom, there had to be at least ten Jewish men for there to be a synagogue. Evidently, there were not even ten practicing Jewish men who believed in God and likely no one at all who knew that Jesus was the Son of God and the Savior of the world.

Philippi was a frontier mission field where the Church was planted with the seeds of these three dramatic conversions. It was the first recorded place that the gospel was preached on European soil!

God, in His foreknowledge, knew that in about two decades (from AD 49 to AD 70), the Jews from Israel would be scattered in mass around the world and into Europe after the Roman destruction of Jerusalem. During that exile, many Christians would also be scattered throughout Europe. In His perfect timing, God established a church both to reach new European converts and to prepare for the coming diaspora (exile) of His people.

A few months ago, a friend of mine was passing through customs in a predominantly Muslim country. It was obvious to her that there were very few Christians (if any) surrounding her. She described it as, at first intimidating, and then exhilarating to realize that she was carrying the Person of the Holy Spirit, God Himself within her into a land of spiritual darkness. Think about how Paul and his companions must have felt entering Europe for the first time with the power of the gospel of Jesus Christ and the presence of the Holy Spirit. They were about to ignite a new continent on fire for God! How awesome to be involved in a new work of God!

🐚 Who are the first three people God converts or "recruits" to start the church in Philippi (verses 13-34)?

🐚 A foreign businesswoman/widow, a possessed slave girl, and a jailer – What do you think about God's chosen combination to start the European church?

🐚 What does this tell you about God and the people He chooses to use?

🐚 **Each of these new believers was in bondage. Lydia was in bondage to Jewish law. The slave girl was in physical and spiritual bondage to her masters and to the powers of darkness. The jailer was in bondage to Roman law (he thought he would be killed for losing his prisoners). How did God set each of them free?**

NOTE ON LYDIA

Lydia was from the city of Thyatira (located in modern-day Turkey), the carpet-making capital of the world, where the art of dying cloth was well practiced. There was a Jewish settlement in Thyatira where Lydia likely became a practicing Jew or worshipper of God. We do not know why Lydia moved to Philippi or whether or not she had a husband. The fact that there is no mention of a man and she seems to make the decisions for her household and earns a living for her household, suggests that she may be a widow. She also appears to be a widow of some means, given the fact that she insists Paul and his guests stay in her home. It appears that the church of Philippi first met in her home. **She is the first European convert to Christianity.**

🐚 Ironically, Paul and Silas also get put in bondage for helping others become free. How does God miraculously set them free?

✺ Describe a time when God set you free and your "chains came loose" (verse 26)?

✺ What do you have to do to be saved (verses 30-31)?

✺ When did "God open your heart to respond" to His plan of salvation (verse 14)?

✺ Do you have a friend or loved one that you want to pray for right now that God would "open up their heart to respond" to His free gift of salvation? Write their names here and claim it by faith!

✺ What happened immediately after people believed Paul's message (verses 15 and 33)?

✺ What opposition was there to starting the church in Philippi?

🐚 *What miracles happened to enable the birth of this new church?*

🐚 *Joy becomes an early theme in the church of Philippi. How did Paul and Silas demonstrate **joy in suffering** (verses 22-25)?*

🐚 *How did Lydia demonstrate **joy in serving** (verses 15 and 40)?*

🐚 *How did the jailer demonstrate **joy in believing** (verse 34)?*

🐚 *Later the Philippian church will become known for its **joy in giving** (Philippians 4). Who were the first people to make sacrifices (giving of their time, energy, talent, finances and even suffering) for the church in Philippi?*

Let's Get Real

What sacrifices have others made to help you grow in Christ? Has God ever prepared a church, group of believers or a providential relationship to be on your journey at just the right time? Tell that story!

What sacrifices are you currently making to help reach others with the message of Christ?

What is the one thing you could do this week to draw closer to Jesus?

What areas of your life do you still need the "chains to come loose?"

JOURNAL RESPONSE

(Take a moment to reflect on Who God is and write a response to Him).

God, You are so…

God, thank you for the time You…

God, forgive me for…

God, help me to …

God, I will trust You to…

PRAYER FROM JEN

When I Need a Miracle!

Dear Daddy,

Thank you for showing me that You never waste a tear or a trial. You promise to work all things for my good. Thank you that nothing is impossible for You! I know You delight when we believe You for miracles. You spoke the world into existence. You are the Almighty Creator, the Alpha and Omega, the Beginning and the End. You hold the whole world in Your hands. You orchestrate every detail of my life. Lord, today I need Your supernatural power. I am trusting You to act on my behalf. Amen!

Lord, do something that only You can do!

"And we know that all things work together for the good of those who love him, who have been called according to his purpose."
Romans 8:28

"Don't follow your
dreams this year, ask
God to fulfill
His dreams through you.
When we can't, God CAN!
When you don't
know what to do,
God will do it for you!"

- JEN

WEEK 2

Joy In
Suffering

WEEK 2 VIDEO NOTES

"...Ask and you will receive, and your joy will be full" (John 16:24).

Joy is an unlimited, renewable resource!
(Isaiah 29:19, Psalm 30:5, Nehemiah 8:10)

Paul introduces himself as a _____ of Christ Jesus.

The Greek word for servant is "doulos" which means _____.

Note: During this time in the Roman empire, 1/4-1/3 of the people were slaves because they couldn't pay their debts. They would have identified with the word slave. Christianity came and broke the power of slavery. Being a slave to Christ meant they had worth and value, because now they were a child of the King and an heir to the Kingdom of heaven.

Everything we go through in life is all about the Gospel.
What are you chained to every day?

Philippians 1:21-25
Would Paul rather live or die?

This life is just a dot!!
"...For what is your life? It is even a _____ that appears for a little time and then vanishes away" (James 4:14).

Change your perspective!
We only have a short time to tell people about Jesus!!

Joy In Suffering

Have you ever been in your house when suddenly the electricity goes out? One minute there is all the commotion and noise of the TV, microwave, dishwasher and vacuum cleaner. Then, without warning, comes silence and darkness. It doesn't matter how many times you turn the light switch or the breaker on and off, there is nothing you can do to get the electricity to come back on. You have to wait. The source of energy that runs all of those lights and appliances does not come from you. It comes from the power company. The exciting news is that God is our power company! We don't have to produce energy on our own. He is our source of power. Acts 1:8 says "you will receive power when the Holy Spirit comes on you…"

The secret to having joy in the midst of suffering is found in the source. Before we break open Philippians, Chapter 1, there are some things we must know deep in our souls about joy:

1. Joy is a Gift…and we aren't the Source.
John 16:24 – You haven't done this before. Ask, using my name, and you will receive, and you will have abundant joy (NLT).

Ecclesiastes 2:26 – God gives wisdom, knowledge and joy…(NLT).

Joy doesn't come from us. Joy doesn't come from our circumstances. We don't have to will ourselves to act happy or wait for a good hair day. Joy is a GIFT that comes from God! All we have to do is ask for it. We need to let this sink in before we start feeling guilty that Paul can be joyful in a foreign prison and we're struggling to be joyful in comfortable suburbia. We aren't the source of joy. Our circumstances aren't the source of joy. Our environment is not the source of joy. What we have or don't have is not the source of joy. Those things might be the source of temporary happiness, but they aren't the source of lasting joy. Joy is a gift that we can ask for every day!

2. Joy is a Fruit…and we aren't the Source.

Galatians 5:22-23 - But the fruit of the Spirit is love, joy, peace, patience, kindness, goodness, faithfulness, gentleness and self-control. Against such things there is no law.

Nehemiah 12:43 - And on that day they offered great sacrifices, rejoicing because God had given them great joy.

Joy is a fruit, and we don't produce it. Did you catch the order of joy in these verses? We don't earn joy, create joy or increase joy by our behavior. No! Joy doesn't follow rules or get explained by laws. There is nothing we can do to deserve it! In Nehemiah, they didn't offer sacrifices to get joy. God gave them joy first, and then they offered sacrifices in gratitude for what God had already produced in them! **I want you to know up front that joy doesn't come from what we do; it comes from Who lives in us.**

Plus, the great thing about a fruit is that it comes back again and again. There may be seasons of dormancy or pruning, but an apple tree will always produce apples again the next fall, no matter how ugly it gets during winter.

3. Joy is an Unlimited Renewable Resource… and (you guessed it) WE AREN'T THE SOURCE!

Isaiah 29:19 - The humble will be filled with fresh joy from the Lord (NLT).

Psalm 30:5 - Weeping may last through the night, but joy comes with the morning (NLT).

Psalm 16:11 - You make known to me the path of life; you will fill me with joy in your presence, with eternal pleasures at your right hand.

Joy isn't limited by our behavior, attitude or resources, because that's just it—we aren't the source. God is our source of joy, and He is unlimited. He is overflowing, never-ending and always able to refill our cup of joy.

But – and this is a big BUT – we have to be ready for this. We may not understand why at first. I guarantee we won't like it at first. BUT…**often the path to unlimited, renewable joy runs smack dab through the middle of a place called suffering.**

Don't put this book down!!!

Listen to what Nehemiah says, "Don't be dejected and sad, for the joy of the Lord is your strength" (Nehemiah 8:10, NLT)!

The joy of our circumstances is not our strength. The joy "of the Lord" is our strength. He alone is our source of joy! And maybe we would never recognize that joy came from Him unless our circumstances were bad enough for us to have no other way of explaining where our joy comes from besides the Almighty, supernatural hand of God. One last thing…

John 16:22 says, "So you have sorrow now, but I will see you again; then you will rejoice, and no one can rob you of that joy" (NLT).

When we aren't our own source of joy, no one can take it away from us. When we aren't the source, we can't run out. When we walk through the fire and come out with joy, we will have finally figured out how to tap into God's reserves. This kind of joy can never be taken away. It's a gift. It's a fruit. It's unlimited. And (I can't believe I'm saying this, but I am) it's worth suffering for.

"The *victory* is greater than the suffering.
We must have an *expectation* of what God is going to do."
-JEN

Take a Look: Philippians 1:3-11

Thanksgiving Prayer

³ I thank my God every time I remember you. ⁴ In all my prayers for all of you, I always pray with joy ⁵ because of your partnership in the gospel from the first day until now, ⁶ being confident of this, that he who began a good work in you will carry it on to completion until the day of Christ Jesus. ⁷ It is right for me to feel this way about all of you, since I have you in my heart and, whether I am in chains or defending and confirming the gospel, all of you share in God's grace with me. ⁸ God can testify how I long for all of you with the affection of Christ Jesus. ⁹ And this is my prayer: that your love may abound more and more in knowledge and depth of insight, ¹⁰ so that you may be able to discern what is best and may be pure and blameless for the day of Christ, ¹¹ filled with the fruit of righteousness that comes through Jesus Christ—to the glory and praise of God.

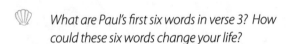 What are Paul's first six words in verse 3? How could these six words change your life?

NOTE ON THE GOSPEL

The word "gospel" literally means "good news." It is derived from the Greek word *angelos* and is closely related to both the "message" and the "messenger." In classical Greek, an euangelos was the person who brought news of a personal or political victory that resulted in great joy. Paul himself defines the gospel as the message that *"Christ died for our sins according to the Scriptures, and that He was buried, and that He rose again the third day"* (1 Corinthians 15:1-4). It is good news because the forgiveness of sins and right standing with God is offered freely and received by faith alone. In short, the gospel is the total sum of the plan of salvation accomplished by the death, burial and resurrection of Jesus Christ.

What are the last five words of verse 4? Would you say that you pray more with complaints or demands or joy?

In verse 5, Paul says that he is joyful because of the Philippians' partnership in the gospel. If the gospel is the death, burial and resurrection of Jesus, what two things have to happen before there is a resurrection?

How does this "partnership in the gospel" idea impact your view of suffering?

Verse 6 is an incredible promise – "He who began a good work in you will carry it on until completion…" What role do you think suffering might play in our "completion?" **What might we be lacking without suffering?**

In verse 10, Paul prays for the Philippians to grow in knowledge and insight so they would be able to: 1. Discern what is best, and 2. Be filled with the fruit of righteousness. How do you grow in knowledge and insight? Is it something you can learn without experience? Would those two benefits be worth the growing pains of experience?

"Discerning what is best" is more than just knowing the difference between right and wrong. Paul wanted them to have God's wisdom. Journal his prayer from verses 9-11 in your own words for yourself and your family:

Let's Get Real

"Consider it pure joy, my brothers and sisters, whenever you face trials of many kinds, because you know that the testing of your faith produces perseverance. Let perseverance finish its work so that you may be mature and complete, not lacking anything" (James 1:2-4).

🐚 *Do you think you can be complete in Christ without suffering?*

🐚 *Do you know someone who is a mature Christian? Have they been through suffering or trials? How do you know they are mature?*

🐚 *Are you willing to go through the pain of the death and burial to get to the benefits of the resurrection?*

🐚 *Has there ever been a time in your life when you have benefited from suffering? Tell your story.*

🐚 *God's plan is usually harder than we would choose. But it is also usually greater than we could ever imagine. If you could turn back time, would you change God's plan?*

When we go through suffering and continue to get out of bed and praise God, it encourages others that they can do the same. There is an elderly man who walks in my neighborhood almost every day. He catches my attention every time because he is hunched over so badly that he is bent forward at the waist and his chest is completely parallel with the ground. He can't even look up and make eye contact. He walks one step at a time staring at the ground. The first time I saw him, I wanted to cry because it looked like he was in so much pain! I thought, *It would be much easier for him to stay at home in bed.*

Then I realized, *If he can do it, so can I!* Now I smile and sing a praise song every time I see him. His tenacity and determination encourages me to keep pressing on. Whatever emotional or physical struggle I have that day, I can still take one more step!

I want to take a moment to acknowledge that some of us might be suffering right now or in pain every day. It might be physical pain or emotional pain. It could be the loss of a loved one, loss of a job, the heartbreak of a wayward child, a broken family or broken dreams. God is not far away. He is walking next to you holding your hand. You are never alone! Cry out to Him and ask Him for what you need today. He is waiting to come to your rescue.

I pray that you will feel God wrap His arms of love around you and hear Him whisper in your ear today: "For I am the Lord your God who takes hold of your right hand and says to you, Do not fear; I will help you" (Isaiah 41:13). If God allows you to go through something painful or hard, it doesn't mean He doesn't love you. He is going to use you in far greater ways than you ever dreamed possible. He can do exceedingly, abundantly more than all you ask or imagine!

Would You Change Your Story?

If you've read our *Miracle for Jen* book or heard us tell our story, you know my daughter has a traumatic brain injury from an accident caused by a drunk driver. Jen was in a coma for six weeks and has been fighting to regain her quality of life ever since. She has suffered more than any mom would ever choose and still suffers every day. I remember a couple years after the accident a news reporter from *NBC Today* asked her if she could change her story would she? During that season of her recovery, she could hardly answer a question without a prompt from me. So I was shocked by her immediate response: "I wouldn't change a single thing. If it wasn't for the accident, I wouldn't know God and need Him the way I do. Besides, if just one person accepts Christ because of my story, it's all worth it. I am so honored that God chose me."

A few minutes later, the news reporter asked me the same question. With tears streaming down my face I said, "Yes, I would change it if I could. No mom would choose to watch her child suffer and be in pain every day. I would do anything to take her place." Since that day, God has changed my heart, and I now realize that God's plan is far greater though different than my plan. He is using Jen in ways we never dreamed possible to lead thousands of people to Jesus. In her weakness, God is strong. Because of her disabilities, God is giving her a platform to share the gospel all over the world! Is it easy? No! But I am so thankful for the promise in 2 Corinthians 12:9, "My grace is sufficient for you, for my power is made perfect in weakness."

Take a Look: Philippians 1:12-26

Paul's Chains Advance the Gospel

¹² Now I want you to know, brothers and sisters, that what has happened to me has actually served to advance the gospel. ¹³ As a result, it has become clear throughout the whole palace guard and to everyone else that I am in chains for Christ. ¹⁴ And because of my chains, most of the brothers and sisters have become confident in the Lord and dare all the more to proclaim the gospel without fear.¹⁵ It is true that some preach Christ out of envy and rivalry, but others out of goodwill. ¹⁶ The latter do so out of love, knowing that I am put here for the defense of the gospel. ¹⁷ The former preach Christ out of selfish ambition, not sincerely, supposing that they can stir up trouble for me while I am in chains. ¹⁸ But what does it matter? The important thing is that in every way, whether from false motives or true, Christ is preached. And because of this I rejoice. Yes, and I will continue to rejoice, ¹⁹ for I know that through your prayers and God's provision of the Spirit of Jesus Christ what has happened to me will turn out for my deliverance. ²⁰ I eagerly expect and hope that I will in no way be ashamed, but will have sufficient courage so that now as always Christ will be exalted in my body, whether by life or by death. ²¹ For to me, to live is Christ and to die is gain. ²² If I am to go on living in the body, this will mean fruitful labor for me. Yet what shall I choose? I do not know! ²³ I am torn between the two: I desire to depart and be with Christ, which is better by far; ²⁴ but it is more necessary for you that I remain in the body. ²⁵ Convinced of this, I know that I will remain, and I will continue with all of you for your progress and joy in the faith, ²⁶ so that through my being with you again your boasting in Christ Jesus will abound on account of me.

 According to verse 12, what was the purpose of Paul's suffering?

This purpose was not only clear to Paul, but it was also clear to another group of people. Who were they?

Paul was chained to a Roman guard. To whom or what are you chained every day? What do you do every day? What is your divine appointment?

How did Paul's suffering help or encourage others (verse 14)?

How might your suffering result in "confidence in the Lord" (verse 14)?

NOTE ON THE ROMAN GUARD

During this first extended imprisonment in Rome, Paul earned the respect and admiration of the elite Praetorian guard who supervised his imprisonment. Nevertheless, he was still wearing chains and most likely chained to a Roman soldier 24/7. The guards would have changed shifts every six hours. With four guards a day for two years, that meant **Paul had 2,920 opportunities to share Jesus face to face (literally) with a member of the Roman guard.** Those guards who heard or received his message would have potentially been deployed all over the Roman Empire. Paul was impacting the world with the gospel of Christ while stuck in his jail cell!

Advancing the Gospel through Cancer

Being in prison, most people would want to give up. Paul saw it as an opportunity to share Jesus. Paul didn't waste the time he was in prison. Our circumstances are not as important as how we respond. How we respond to suffering, reveals what is in our heart and what we truly believe. "For the mouth speaks what the heart is full of" (Matthew 12:34). That is why it is so important to hide God's Word in our heart, so when trials come we are ready. This past winter, my husband Andy and I were in Atlanta for seven weeks while he got radiation treatments for prostate cancer. Every day Andy was "chained" to walking into the clinic for radiation. So he shared his faith with the nurses, doctors and anyone who would listen. God even allowed us to share Jesus with all the cancer patients staying at the Hope Lodge. If we were stuck there, we were going to make the best of it and look for new ways for God to use us.

Look for ways to share Jesus wherever you are. Instead of a pity party, turn it around and say, "Who can I help or encourage today?" **Your pain has a purpose! It makes you passionate to reach out and help others.**

 Paul's friends and enemies are preaching about Christ. Even though both groups have different motives, what is the end result (verse 18)? What brings Paul joy (verse 18)?

Many people serve God for the wrong reasons. Paul knew some were preaching to build their own reputations. Regardless of their motive, Paul rejoiced that the gospel was being preached. This is a great example for us to follow. Often we are tempted to take our eyes off Jesus and focus on what others are doing wrong. God is the one who judges the motives of the heart. Paul could have bashed these preachers, but he did not. His primary focus was to spread the Gospel.

Have you ever been tempted to criticize another preacher or ministry that you believe you have a reason to disrespect? What can you learn from Paul's example about how to treat other leaders or co-laborers?

According to verse 19, what two things are sustaining Paul during his imprisonment?

Do you think God granted Paul a greater provision of the Holy Spirit because of his suffering?

According to verses 20-25, would Paul rather live or die? Who benefits if he lives and who benefits if he dies?

What does Paul say in verse 25 that makes you think he already knows what is going to happen?

What evidence is there in this passage that Paul is more focused on others than on himself during this ordeal?

"I Knew in My Spirit"

I love this! Paul already knows in his spirit what will happen before it happens. By the mystery of the grace of God, Paul was given clarity in the midst of suffering about his future.

The night of our car wreck, my daughter Jen had a Glasgow Coma Scale (GCS is how doctors measure your consciousness) of 3, and dead people are a 3! No one thought she would live through the night. But somehow, in my heart, I knew she would live. God had given me an unexplainable peace. The next morning, a friend brought me a verse of Scripture that said, "This sickness will not end in death; no, it is for God's glory that God's Son may be glorified" (John 11:4). I knew in my spirit that God was speaking to me and giving me the faith to believe it. Even though the doctors could not give me any confirmations, God had already given me all the confirmation I needed.

Let's Get Real

Have you ever been in so much pain that you longed for heaven? Read Revelation 21:4-5 and write it here:

Paul says in the midst of his trials that "the important thing" is that "Christ is preached." When you are going through trials, what is important to you?

Has your suffering ever given you a chance to tell someone else about Jesus? Did that bring you joy? Tell your story.

Choose How to Travel

My friend Helene battled colon cancer for several years. She came to our ladies' Bible study every week and her face always glowed with the joy of the Lord. When she became too weak to walk, I went to visit her in the hospital and I will never forget what she said to me. In fact I wrote it down on a sticky note.

"We don't get to choose the journey, but we do choose how we travel through it. I choose to travel in grace, mercy and trust. I pray countless lives are touched everywhere in between!"

Helene shared Jesus with all the doctors, hospital staff, her neighbors and everyone she came in contact with until the day she was completely healed in heaven. That is exactly how I want to be!

If I'm honest, it's sometimes tempting for me to look at others and think, *I want their journey instead of mine. Their journey looks easier!* That's when I have to stop and trust God's plan and know that He is the potter and I am the clay. He is molding each of us and shaping us into who He wants us to be. He is working all things for our good! His plan for our lives is far greater than our plan! It may not be easier or comfortable, but it will be greater for His Kingdom purposes!

> *C.S. Lewis said, "Pain is God's megaphone." Often God uses pain to get you to listen to Him or to get others to listen to you. Either way, suffering expands your voice. Who have you gained influence with because of your suffering that you would not have previously been able to relate to?*

> *It was the provision of the Holy Spirit and the prayers of others that sustained Paul during his long ordeal. Who do you know suffering today that you can pray for? Pray for them now.*

> *Did it give you joy to focus on someone else for a moment? I know it always gives me joy when I focus on helping others instead of being consumed with my own problems.*

Syrian Refugees

Our family has a dear Lebanese friend who helps lead a Christian church in Beirut. Recently our friend Diana was telling us about the Syrian refugees flooding into Lebanon. They fled their homes to escape the dangers of war and famine only to beg and suffer severe illness on the streets in foreign countries. In Lebanon, where there are only four million residents, they now have an additional two million Syrian refugees. It's more than the small government can handle. It was heartbreaking to hear how these mothers and children have lost everything, many of them separated from family members and forced into prostitution.

Diana and her family help organize relief efforts to provide humanitarian aid. She comes face to face with the suffering of these refugees and their devastating stories every day. I asked her how she handled watching such suffering and never having enough to go around. She explained that the suffering is unimaginable but the work of God among these refuges is equally unimaginable. The gospel is spreading through visions, dreams and miracles much like the New Testament times. Diana told us how every day many Syrians are being baptized and believing the good news of salvation--news they would not have likely heard or been free to receive in Syria. This is just one more modern-day example of how God uses suffering to advance the gospel. While God is not the cause of suffering, He will always use it for good for those who love Him (Romans 8:28).

Take a Look: Philippians 1:27-30

Stand Firm in the Spirit

[27] *Whatever happens, conduct yourselves in a manner worthy of the gospel of Christ. Then, whether I come and see you or only hear about you in my absence, I will know that you stand firm in the one Spirit, striving together as one for the faith of the gospel* [28] *without being frightened in any way by those who oppose you. This is a sign to them that they will be destroyed, but that you will be saved—and that by God.* [29] *For it has been granted to you on behalf of Christ not only to believe in him, but also to suffer for him,* [30] *since you are going through the same struggle you saw I had, and now hear that I still have.*

 What is a "manner worthy of the gospel?" When did Paul encourage the Christians in Philippi to conduct themselves in that manner?
This question is very convicting for me. Do I conduct myself in a manner worthy of the gospel? Sometimes I ask myself, **When people look at my life, do they want what I have? Do I have joy? Do my children and my neighbors want what I have?**

What is Paul's advice for dealing with opposition (verse 28)?

Who is the source of salvation? What was one sign of salvation (verse 28)?

How does Paul describe suffering (verse 29)?

Enduring faith through trials shouts to others that God is real. It encourages others not to give up. Suffering gets our focus off of earthly things and on to eternal things that last forever. When we suffer, we experience God in greater ways. We feel His arms of love wrap around us, and we are completely dependent on Him. This is right where He wants us, dependent on Him instead of our own strength.

How was Paul able to relate to the Philippian Christians because of his suffering (verse 30)?

Let's Get Real

◈ *Describe a time when you did not behave in a "manner worthy of the gospel" in the midst of suffering?*

◈ *Have you ever witnessed someone who did behave in a manner worthy of the gospel in the midst of suffering? What impact did their testimony have on you?*

One of my dear friends, Joni Eareckson Tada, says: "My weakness, that is, my quadriplegia, is my greatest asset because it forces me into the arms of Christ every single morning when I get up." Joni has a ministry called Joni and Friends that has touched millions with the gospel all over the world. She was instrumental in encouraging our family to start the Hope Out Loud ministry.

◈ *Paul speaks of suffering as a privilege—"It has been granted to you"—as if you just received a reward. In what way could suffering be viewed as a reward or a privilege?*

◈ *How could suffering be a gift with a purpose?*

Dancing in the Rain

Years ago in a neighborhood Bible study, I met a precious friend named Ann. She was elderly and had been through much pain in her lifetime. Ann was a delight to be around because she was always full of joy and wisdom. She loved to tell people about Jesus and she shared her story often. Friends would drive her to speak all over the east coast. Her husband was murdered on a business trip and it remained a mystery. No one was ever convicted for the crime. If that wasn't enough suffering, Ann was also legally blind. Through it all, God was her faithful companion and her stronghold.

The last time I visited with her, she was battling cancer. We prayed together and then I said. "Ann, what advice do you have for me?" She smiled and said, "Learn to dance in the rain. Don't wait for the storm to pass. Every step in life is preparing us to meet the King and to be more like Him. The only thing that really matters is what have you done with Jesus? And where are you going to spend eternity?" That was the last time I saw Ann; she went home to meet her King face to face. Every time I am struggling to make it through the day, I picture Ann dancing on streets of gold and I smile and say, "Today I choose to dance in the rain!"

ACTION STEP
TAKE A MOMENT TO SEND AN EMAIL OR A TEXT TO SOMEONE LIKE ANN WHO HAS ENCOURAGED YOU BY SUFFERING "IN A MANNER WORTHY OF THE GOSPEL." DON'T LET THE SUN GO DOWN TODAY BEFORE YOU THANK THAT PERSON FOR BEING A ROLE MODEL OF HOW TO SUFFER WELL!

JOURNAL RESPONSE

(Take a moment to reflect on Who God is and write a response to Him).

God, thank You for the way You…

God, You are so…

God, forgive me for…

God, help me to …

God, I will trust You to…

PRAYER FROM JEN

When I Need to be Carried!

Dear Comforter,

When I woke up today, I felt like I couldn't take another step. Thank you for whispering to me…"I have made you and I will sustain you; I will CARRY you and I will rescue you." Lord, I love the poem about the footprints in the sand. When there was only one set of footprints during the hard times, those were Your footprints, because You were carrying me. Thank you for knowing when I can't take another step on my own. Amen!

You always catch me when I fall!

"The Lord is good, a refuge in times of trouble. He cares for those who trust in him." Nahum 1:7

WEEK 3

Joy In Serving

WEEK 3 VIDEO NOTES

Plug into the Power Source!
(Acts 1:8, John 7:38-39)

What Brings Joy?

1. Spending Time with Jesus - Do you have a secret place?

2. Singing _____ _____ (Psalm 16:11, Psalm 71:23)

3. Reading God's Word

4. _____ God's Word   (John 15:10-11)

5. _____ _____ Produces Joy (Galatians 5:22)

6. A Thankful Heart

7. _____ Others

Jesus is our best example of humility and obedience.
Philippians 2:5-11

Jesus did not cease to be God during His earthly ministry. But He did set aside His heavenly glory of a face-to-face relationship with God. He also set aside His independent authority. During His earthly ministry, Christ completely submitted Himself to the will of the Father.

Joy In Serving

In 2006, the women's ministry leader at our church recruited me to lead our Tuesday morning Bible study that hundreds of women attend weekly. I had led small group Bible studies in my home for many years and never had any aspirations beyond women falling in love with God's Word and experiencing His presence in my home. I had no idea what God was setting me up for, or setting up for me.

Two months before that term began, the accident happened. In the initial stages of suffering, you tend to go into survival mode. It took every ounce of strength I had just to survive each day. My daughter was in a coma 90 miles away. My husband was in a hospital in another city and undergoing multiple surgeries. I was in a wheelchair with no use of my left arm or leg. And my son was supposed to be attending school and turning in homework. I remember being completely overwhelmed because he had a science fair project due. (I admit – I was one of those moms who always micro-managed his school projects). But now I was thinking, I cannot possibly add one more thing to my plate! There were pills to take every hour, doctors' appointments, therapy visits, insurance battles, and the overwhelming uncertainty that my daughter may not wake up. And to top it off, I couldn't even stay with Jen overnight because of my injuries. Every day, I made the three-hour round trip just to be with her for a few hours, and then did it all over the next day!

Now, I should insert here that I was extremely blessed to have an army of people helping me. I never could have survived without them. Every day someone came to bathe and dress me and drive me to the UVA children's hospital. While I was gone, other friends came to clean my house, do my laundry and leave dinner on my doorstep. And there were precious moments when God Himself wrapped His arms around me and poured out His peace and comfort in unexplainable ways I never would have known without these trials. If you have suffered and had God pick you up and carry you through a season or send a friend for you to lean on, you know what I'm talking about. Nevertheless, I was just barely surviving.

Three months later, Jen came home from the hospital but she still had so many problems. She had a feeding tube and no short-term memory. Jen screamed in the shower because her body was hypersensitive, and she didn't like anyone touching her. She could not get dressed or do anything by herself. A nurse came to our house every day to help us. I was still in a wheelchair, and the nerves in my left arm were severed so I couldn't use my left hand. I felt helpless as a mom! I couldn't administer Jen's feeding tube, much less bathe her or walk her up the stairs to her bedroom. Several months later, a few close friends said, "Linda, we really think you should still lead that Bible study. It might be good for you to get out of the house one day a week." At first, I thought my friends were crazy! However, the more I prayed about it, I knew it was exactly what God wanted me to do.

That first Tuesday, I hopped on one leg across the stage to the podium and sat in a chair while the women had their eyes closed during prayer. I wasn't about to have someone carry my wheelchair up the steps and onto the stage. **I don't remember what I said, but I remember at that moment God was calling me to live my pain out publicly for the benefit of others.** Afterwards, tons of women came and told me that just seeing me out of the house gave them hope to persevere. **That was the day I learned the difference between surviving and thriving…it was found in a thing called "serving."**

God filled me with joy as I focused on helping others instead of being consumed with my own problems. As I said before, most of us would never choose our suffering. And yet, suffering opens doors for us to experience the power and Person of God in higher ways than we ever thought possible. But that miraculous comfort is not meant for us just to savor for ourselves; it's meant for us to share with others.

Paul says: "Praise be to the God and Father of our Lord Jesus Christ, the Father of compassion and the God of all comfort, who comforts us in all our troubles, so that we can comfort those in any trouble with the comfort we ourselves receive from God. For just as we share abundantly in the sufferings of Christ, so also our comfort abounds through Christ. If we are distressed, it is for your comfort and salvation; if we are comforted, it is for your comfort…" (2 Corinthians 1:3-6).

True, joy comes through suffering, but an even greater joy comes through serving others out of our suffering. The first chapter of Philippians basically ends with "I know you are suffering, but…" The second chapter begins with "It's time for us to stop looking out for ourselves and start looking out for others." In other words, it's time for us to stop surviving and start thriving. It's time for our pain to have a purpose. It's time for us to serve others.

There is an old hymn that says, "There is joy in serving Jesus, joy that triumphs over pain…Joy that throbs within my heart every moment, every hour…There is joy in serving Jesus."

Take a Look: Philippians 2:1-4

Having the Mind of Christ

¹ *Therefore if you have any encouragement from being united with Christ, if any comfort from his love, if any common sharing in the Spirit, if any tenderness and compassion,* ² *then make my joy complete by being like-minded, having the same love, being one in spirit and of one mind.* ³ *Do nothing out of selfish ambition or vain conceit. Rather, in humility value others above yourselves,* ⁴ *not looking to your own interests but each of you to the interests of the others.*

 In verses 3 and 4, what shift in behavior, thoughts and attitude is Paul calling the church of Philippi to live out?

When I read verses 3 and 4, I automatically think of my precious mother-in-law, Fran. She is selfless and gets the greatest joy from meeting the needs of others. She enjoys being the "hands and feet of Jesus." Fran has the gift of serving and she often notices my needs even before I do. Serving does not come easy for me. I love to exhort and encourage people with prayers and Scriptures through a text, card or phone call. I wouldn't, however, spontaneously think to clean their house or take out their trash unless they asked me for help. I want to serve, but I have to make a conscious effort to serve. It doesn't just naturally happen. Even if serving is not our greatest spiritual gift, it is something God commands us to do. Joshua 22:5 says, "…serve him with all your heart and with all your soul." God wants us to serve in our church, our families and our communities. He also wants us to reach out and help those in need.

 According to verse 1, what things equip you to serve others (hint: there are five)?

According to the text, where do those five things come from?

Here's the important thing: Do any of those five things have anything to do with your talents, abilities or capacity to perform? What does that tell you about what God expects as a prerequisite for serving others?

Let's Get Real:

 In your opinion, what qualifies you to serve? In God's opinion, what qualifies you to serve? Whose opinion are you listening to?

 One of my favorite quotes says, "God qualifies the unqualified." Has that ever been true in your life? Tell about a time God called you to do something you felt inadequate to accomplish? How did God equip you?

I believe that God delights in asking us to do things we are incapable of in our own strength. Why? Because He gets all the glory!

 In verse 2, Paul calls the believers in Philippi to be unified and have the same:

> *Mind (like-minded)*
> *Heart (same love)*
> *Spirit (one in spirit)*
> *Purpose (one mind)*

Which one of these areas is your biggest battleground? How do you claim victory in that area?

Do you need to confess and repent losing the battle in one of these areas? How does losing the battle for your mind, heart, spirit or purpose affect your joy?

Confession

My biggest battleground is my mind. Thoughts of inadequacy and negativity are my greatest obstacle in serving. I would miss the joy of helping many people if I obeyed my thoughts. What helps me is picturing "taking captive every thought to the obedience of Christ" (2 Corinthians 10:5). I literally wallpaper the walls in my house with sticky notes that have the Word of God on them. I write down God's truth and speak it out loud over and over until I get victory over my negative thoughts.

Every Tuesday when I went to church to lead Bible study, I carried sticky notes in my purse with my favorite verses that gave me courage and strength. Whenever I started to feel inadequate or overwhelmed, I would claim the promises of God's Word out loud and tell Satan he had no power over me. Every day I have to choose truth and refuse to believe the lies of the enemy that I'm not worthy or not smart enough. I don't have to be talented or good enough because God promises that in my weakness, He will be strong.

After our wreck, my daughter Jen had terrible anxiety and could not walk into a room full of people or even into a waiting room at the doctor's office. I wrote 2 Timothy 1:7, "For God has not given us a spirit of fear, but of power, and of love and a sound mind" on a sticky note, and we took it with us everywhere we went. Some days we would quote it out loud 20 times just to survive the day. Jen loves God with all her heart and whenever she would say that verse out loud, God gave her the courage she needed to take the next step. God's Word is alive and powerful! It breaks the stronghold of fear! Soon, Jen was able to speak in front of large crowds and share her story to encourage others with her child-like faith. It was unbelievable! **One day I asked her, "How can you get on stage in front of thousands of people and not be afraid?" She smiled and said, "It's easy! I picture Jesus standing in the back of the room, and I'm just talking to Him!"**

Jesus: The Ultimate Servant

Philippians 2:5-11 is the most widely discussed and famously debated passage in the entire book! Before you read it, ask God to open your eyes and your heart to see and hear what He wants you to see and hear. Ask Him to help you understand "what really matters" about this passage for your life today. Ask Him to give you the "same mindset as Jesus Christ."

> "The Son of Man did not come to be served but to serve
> and to give His life as a ransom for many" (Matthew 20:28; Mark 10:45).

Write your prayer here:

_____

_____

_____

_____

_____

Now read this passage carefully and prayerfully 3 times…

Take a Look: Philippians 2:5-11

The Humility and Exaltation of Christ

⁵ In your relationships with one another, have the same mindset as Christ Jesus: ⁶ Who, being in very nature God, did not consider equality with God something to be used to his own advantage; ⁷ rather, he made himself nothing by taking the very nature of a servant, being made in human likeness. ⁸ And being found in appearance as a man, he humbled himself by becoming obedient to death—even death on a cross! ⁹ Therefore God exalted him to the highest place and gave him the name that is above every name, ¹⁰ that at the name of Jesus every knee should bow, in heaven and on earth and under the earth, ¹¹ and every tongue acknowledge that Jesus Christ is Lord, to the glory of God the Father.

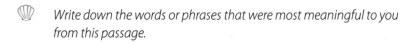 *Write down the words or phrases that were most meaningful to you from this passage.*

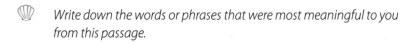 *What do you think God might be trying to say to you right now?*

What phrases in the passage are evidence that Jesus was fully God and not just a man?

NOTE ON INCARNATION

The Incarnation is the belief that Jesus was fully God and fully man at the same time while He lived on earth. When He took upon the form of earthly flesh in a human body, He did not give up His divinity. Instead, He chose not to exercise His rights or privileges as God in order to fulfill the will of His Father and the plan of redemption. At the same time, He was 100% God, He was also 100% man and experienced all of the weaknesses, temptations and pain that we face in the flesh, yet He did not sin.

What phrases serve as evidence that Jesus was fully human as well?

The word Paul chooses to describe Jesus as a "servant" is the same Greek word doulos that Paul used to describe himself in his greeting in Chapter 1. What did that word "doulos" mean? What do you think is the significance of this word choice?

Verse 7 says that Jesus "made himself nothing." How is this act the exact opposite of our human nature? How might this also be more proof that Jesus was fully God?

"Jesus considered his deity an opportunity for service and obedience. His deity became a matter not of getting but of giving, not of being served but of serving, not of dominance but of obedience" (Frank Theilman, The NIV Application Commentary: Philippians, page 129).

Making a Name for Yourself

I have a friend whose daughter attends one of the top 25 high schools in the U.S. Every parent in her area tries to send their children to that elite school. You are almost scorned as a "bad parent" if you don't make preparations for your son or daughter to be accepted. So, of course, my friend Cindy jumped through all the hoops to assure her daughter would have this great educational advantage. Upon acceptance, she attended a parent orientation. At the orientation, the principal expertly advised, "Parents, your children have four years until they attend college. It's time for them to start making a name for themselves. It's time for them to set themselves apart and make their name great!" She said the audience of several hundred parents erupted in applause.

Cindy started to cheer along with them until the Holy Spirit within her corrected her thinking—*Wait a minute,* she thought. *This is not the mind of Christ. This is not what I desire for my daughter. Jesus did not try to make His name great. He made Himself nothing. He brought glory to God, and God made His name great.* Cindy said that right then and there she started praying for her daughter. "I didn't hear another word that principal said," she recounted. "I started doing battle for my daughter's heart and mind. I started begging God to give her the mind of Christ." Each day that her daughter goes to school, Cindy prays the pages of Scripture out loud over her heart, mind, spirit and purpose. She said that her goal is to pray every single page of Scripture over her child during her four years of high school! I love that!

 How would you describe "the mind of Christ?"

 What is the ultimate purpose of having the same mind as Christ (verse 11)?

Let's Get Real

🐚 *How would having the "same mindset as Christ Jesus" help you serve others?*

🐚 *Do you think having the mind of Christ leads to joy or sorrow? Do you have any evidence to support your answer?*

🐚 *Do you think you could ever be fully satisfied following your own mind and pleasing yourself? Do you have any evidence to support this answer?*

🐚 *What can you do today to "make yourself nothing" and "become obedient" to God's plan for you?*

Bowing Before Breakfast

Many years ago, God nudged me to start every day out by literally getting down on my knees and bowing before Him. I was a slave to my To-Do Lists and my calendar. This was a physical reminder to me and to God that I was attempting to empty myself of my desires and open my life up to His will and plan for my day. Bowing is the posture of surrender! I would say out loud "**Lord, I don't want to miss one plan you have for me today. Empty me of all my fears and fill me with Your power today.**" I started to be more aware of God's presence and the divine appointments God had for me each day.

One morning, I overslept. As I was rushing to get ready, I was praying silently as I was getting dressed. God kept speaking to my heart "You need to bow!" It wasn't an audible voice, just a strong urge in my heart and mind. I started to argue with God in my mind, *Lord, why do I need to bow? You know my thoughts. You know I am surrendering to You.* Then as clear as I have ever known anything in my life, I heard God whisper to my heart, **"Because the enemy sees you when you bow and he knows you are surrendered to me for the day!"** I knew that thought was from God, spoken to me through the Holy Spirit that lives within me, because I surely had never realized that truth before. So you guessed it. I stopped, bowed and surrendered my day to God! Don't let the urgent rob you from doing what is most important!

Just now while I was typing, I got a text from one of my dearest friends that said, "I listen to the song "Holy Spirit" by Kari Jobe every morning and evening and sing it out loud on my knees. God is making me so aware of His presence!" We should never try to put God in a box. He is never boring! God is fun and exciting! He is the lover of your soul. Enjoy His presence! We can have freedom to worship Him with no reservations. He longs for us to be completely abandoned to Him. If you ask God, He will reveal Himself to you in new ways. You might even decide to dance in the kitchen with Him tonight as you are washing the dishes.

"Therefore God exalted him to the highest place and gave him the name that is above every name, that at the name of Jesus every knee should bow, in heaven and on earth and under the earth, and every tongue acknowledge that Jesus Christ is Lord, to the glory of God the Father" (Philippians 2:9-11). These verses bring me great joy. The name of Jesus is so powerful. Sometimes when I feel like I'm drowning, I just speak His name out loud and feel better.

Someday, every single person will acknowledge Jesus as Lord. The question is not "Will you acknowledge Jesus as Lord?" but "When will you acknowledge Jesus as Lord?" I'm praying that you will acknowledge Jesus as Lord before you stand before Him so He can be the one making payment for your sin. Have you acknowledged Him as Lord for your salvation?

SALVATION PRAYER

God's Word says, "If you declare with your mouth, 'Jesus is Lord', and believe in your heart that God raised Him from the dead, you will be saved" (Romans 10:9).

God doesn't force us to love Him. If He did, it wouldn't be real love. He gives us a choice. Once you pray and invite Him into your heart and life, His Spirit lives in you and fills you with His power and strength.

If you don't remember a time when you prayed and asked Jesus to be your Savior, you can pray a prayer today from your heart to God's heart. You don't need fancy words. You just have to realize your need for a Savior. "Everyone who calls on the name of the Lord will be saved" (Romans 10:13).

Jesus died on the cross for you and He loves you so much. Salvation is a free gift of God's grace.

Today, you can pray and become a follower of Jesus Christ.

> Dear God,
>
> I recognize my need for a Savior. I don't want to go through this life on my own any longer. Please come into my heart and life today and forgive me of my sins.
>
> I believe You sent Your Son Jesus to earth to die for me. I believe that You raised Jesus from the dead. I believe that You have power over death. Come into my heart and give me new life. I want to be a follower of Jesus Christ.
>
> Help me to obey You in everything I say and do. I surrender all!
>
> In Jesus Name, Amen!

Angels Are Rejoicing!

If you just prayed that salvation prayer and received Jesus as your Lord and Savior, all of heaven is rejoicing with you! Luke 15:10 says, "...there is rejoicing in the presence of the angels of God over one sinner who repents."

Salvation is a free gift of God's grace. When I picture Jesus hanging on the cross for me, it brings tears to my eyes to think about all the times I fail Him. Yet, Jesus loved me so much! He chose to stay on a rugged cross and pay the penalty for my sins—past, present and future!

The Crucifixion

In Paul's world, death on the cross was the cruelest form of execution in the Roman Empire. Although a Roman citizen could be crucified for the highest form of treason, crucifixion was commonly reserved for the lowest classes, especially slaves. After typically being tortured and nailed to the cross, the victim experienced a slow and humiliating death by blood loss, thirst, and ultimately suffocation. Add to this physical torture, the emotional torture of Jesus being abandoned by His Heavenly Father because He carried the weight and darkness of our sin.

Jesus became separated from His Father so we could be connected to His Father. Close your eyes for a moment and picture Jesus hanging on the cross for you. What do you want to say to Him?

_____

_____

_____

_____

_____

_____

_____

_____

_____

_____

_____

_____

_____

_____

_____

_____

_____

_____

Jesus Is My Everything!

Dear Glorious One,

Wow! You are the perfect Lamb of God who takes away the sins of the world!
I am in awe of who You are! You are the Alpha and the Omega, the Beginning and the
End. You are beyond comprehension. There are not enough words to describe You. You
are the sum of everything! You are my Healer, Redeemer, Provider, and my Best Friend.
You are my Joy and my Strength. You are the One that can fill the deepest longings of
my soul. I can't wait to live with You in heaven where I can worship You for eternity! I
want to shout Your name to the world. I am so honored that You would want to have an
intimate, personal relationship with me.

You complete me!

Love, Jen

Take a Look: Philippians 2:12-18

Shining As Stars

[12] *Therefore, my dear friends, as you have always obeyed—not only in my presence, but now much more in my absence—continue to work out your salvation with fear and trembling,* [13] *for it is God who works in you to will and to act in order to fulfill his good purpose.* [14] *Do everything without grumbling or arguing,* [15] *so that you may become blameless and pure, "children of God without fault in a warped and crooked generation." Then you will shine among them like stars in the sky* [16] *as you hold firmly to the word of life. And then I will be able to boast on the day of Christ that I did not run or labor in vain.* [17] *But even if I am being poured out like a drink offering on the sacrifice and service coming from your faith, I am glad and rejoice with all of you.* [18] *So you too should be glad and rejoice with me.*

🐚 *What word is used to describe God's purpose in verse 13? What does this tell you about God's nature? About suffering? About serving?*

🐚 *How might the description of God's purpose in verse 13 enable Paul to be glad and rejoice even though he is being "poured out like a drink offering (verse 17)?*

🐚 *Have you ever felt drained from serving? What did you do to recover?*

🐚 *Fill in the blanks from verse 13: "For it is God who works in you to _____ and to _____ in order to fulfill His good purpose."*
How can this truth encourage you on a day that you don't feel like serving?

NOTE ON "WORK OUT YOUR SALVATION WITH FEAR AND TREMBLING"

Paul is not advocating salvation by works in verse 12. In the very next verse, he explains that "it is God who works in you." He means for the Philippians (and us) to demonstrate outwardly the work that God has completed inwardly. If God has forgiven us and given us a clean heart, there ought to be external evidence of the work He has done. While the point of belief for salvation delivers us from the penalty of sin, God fully intends for us to be set free daily from the power and presence of sin by the ongoing work of the Holy Spirit.

The Greek word translated "fear" in this context can equally mean "reverence." The Greek word for "work out" means "continually work on bringing something to completion." The idea of "trembling" is a healthy concern of not offending God through disobedience.

What two things could keep you from having joy while serving others (verse 14)?

In verse 15, Paul talks about Christians shining like the stars in a crooked generation. What is the one thing you could do today to be a light to those around you?

"To *shine for Jesus* means to glow so brightly that people have to look at you because they are *drawn* to you."
- Jen

Let's Get Real

How does God's Word give "life?" Tell about a time that God's Word has breathed life into your soul.

ACTION STEP
WRITE PHILIPPIANS 2:13 ON A STICKY NOTE OR NOTE CARD AND PUT IT SOMEWHERE WHERE YOU WILL SEE IT EVERY DAY. ON THE BACK, WRITE PHILIPPIANS 4:13.

Why did Paul say the believers at Philippi should rejoice (verses 17-18)? Why should we rejoice in light of verses 17-18?

Can you think of one person who has been a great example of serving without complaining or arguing? Follow his/her example today!

Being Thankful!

Earlier I mentioned my sister and her family who are church planters. Once when they were moving to a new city to start a church, they asked God to provide a house for them. The house He provided was infested with cockroaches. Not just any cockroaches, these critters were two and three inches long! They crawled over her children at night. They raided her pantry. They multiplied in the laundry. I hate to say it but none of our family wanted to visit because we were afraid to sleep there! She tried not to complain, but inside she grew more and more frustrated with God: "Lord, is this how you treat the people who serve you?" she questioned. A few months later, she was reading *The Hiding Place* to her children and read about the time Corrie Ten Boom thanked God for her lice in prison. The lice had actually protected Corrie from the prison guards. My sister decided to get on her knees with her kids and thank God for the cockroaches. It seemed silly, but she was inspired by Corrie Ten Boom's example to stop complaining and rejoice in everything. The very next day, a friend called and offered them a brand new house (without cockroaches) that was four-times the square footage for half the price!

Take a Look: Philippians 2:19-30

Two Examples of Servants: Timothy and Epaphroditus

19 I hope in the Lord Jesus to send Timothy to you soon, that I also may be cheered when I receive news about you. 20 I have no one else like him, who will show genuine concern for your welfare. 21 For everyone looks out for their own interests, not those of Jesus Christ. 22 But you know that Timothy has proved himself, because as a son with his father he has served with me in the work of the gospel. 23 I hope, therefore, to send him as soon as I see how things go with me. 24 And I am confident in the Lord that I myself will come soon. 25 But I think it is necessary to send back to you Epaphroditus, my brother, co-worker and fellow soldier, who is also your messenger, whom you sent to take care of my needs. 26 For he longs for all of you and is distressed because you heard he was ill. 27 Indeed he was ill, and almost died. But God had mercy on him, and not on him only but also on me, to spare me sorrow upon sorrow. 28 Therefore I am all the more eager to send him, so that when you see him again you may be glad and I may have less anxiety. 29 So then, welcome him in the Lord with great joy, and honor people like him, 30 because he almost died for the work of Christ. He risked his life to make up for the help you yourselves could not give me.

 *In what ways is **Timothy** a great example of a servant? What words does Paul use to describe him (verses 20-23)?*

🐚 In what ways is **Epaphroditus** a great example of a servant? What words does Paul use to describe him (verses 25-30)?

🐚 Why did Paul need Timothy to stay with him awhile longer (verse 23)?

🐚 What is Paul once again confident of in verse 24?

🐚 Verse 27 happens to be the verse God gave me the night before my dad underwent open-heart surgery. **It was a comfort to me to know that God does not recklessly heap "sorrow upon sorrow" on us.** What does this verse teach you about God? How does it make you feel? Tuck this one away; you may need it some day!

NOTE ON EPAPHRODITUS

Epaphroditus was the messenger sent by the church of Philippi to bring relief, financial aid and supplies to Paul in prison in Rome. While he was serving Paul in Rome, he became sick and nearly died. God chose to spare his life, and Paul decided to send him back to Philippi so the people who loved him would not lose any more joy worrying about his welfare. It is likely that either Epaphroditus or Timothy carried the letter of Philippians back to the church at Philippi. We should note that again Paul was more concerned with comforting the believers in Philippi than he was with his own comfort, which is why he chose to send Epaphroditus back to them. Paul's greatest "anxiety" seems to be restoring their joy, which may be one of the secrets to his own joy.

Let's Get Real

 Do you know a modern day Timothy or Epaphroditus? Tell his or her story.

Crazy Adventures

My favorite example of a modern day Timothy or Epaphroditus is our friend Lauren. When she was in college, Lauren spent almost every weekend driving Jen and me to speak at different churches up and down the east coast. Lauren was so joyful and honored to help us. She was serving the Lord and she never complained. Those weekend trips were not easy! We had an old GPS and often got lost. (That was before the iPhone). Once in downtown Richmond, the GPS sent us the wrong way down a one-way street and the traffic was coming right toward us. "AHH!!" we all screamed! We had many crazy adventures! Jen's brain was still very injured and she would get sick with headaches and stomach pain in the car. She would need naps and food every couple of hours. Also, because of her short-term memory loss, Jen never knew what day it was or what town we were in.

One night after speaking at a women's event, we came back to the house where we were staying and found literally hundreds, maybe thousands, of flying beetle bugs swarming all over the room. We were in the middle of nowhere, with no hotels, and the people who owned the house were on vacation. I was so worried that Jen would be afraid. Much to my surprise, Jen went straight to bed and prayed, "Lord, help me to sleep with my mouth closed so I don't swallow any bugs." She fell sound asleep before her prayer was done. Lauren, on the other hand, stayed up all night hitting those flying bugs with her slip, while I hid under the covers and tried to sing a praise song. I can still picture it in my mind, and I giggle every time I think of that story!

 How can you be a "Timothy" or "Epaphroditus" today?

 Would you be willing to risk your life for the gospel?

My Friend Linda

Often when I am teaching Bible study on Tuesday mornings, I will come out to my car to drive home and my sweet friend Linda will have surprised me with a homemade meal for my family or a chocolate eclair cake in my back seat. She knows I am not a good cook and a homemade surprise is something I will greatly appreciate. My family is thrilled too because Linda's meals taste much better than mine!

Because the gift of serving doesn't come naturally for me, I would have never thought to bless someone with a surprise meal or homemade dessert in their car. My friend Linda's example of kindness and thoughtfulness has encouraged me to pray and ask God to make me more aware of creative ways I can serve and bless others!

Take a moment to brainstorm and make a list of creative ways that you could bless others.

ACTION STEP

VERSE 29 SAYS TO WELCOME THE LORD'S SERVANTS WITH JOY AND HONOR THEM. MAKE PLANS TO DO SOMETHING THIS WEEK TO HONOR OR SERVE A MODERN-DAY TIMOTHY OR EPAPHRODITUS WHO IS "POURING OUT THEIR LIFE" TO SERVE CHRIST.

_____

_____

_____

_____

_____

_____

_____

_____

JOURNAL RESPONSE

(Take a moment to reflect on Who God is and write a response to Him).

Thank You for the time You…

God, You are so…

God, forgive me for…

God, help me to …

God, I will trust You to…

PRAYER FROM JEN

When I Need to Change!

Dear All-Knowing Father,

I was convicted by a quote that I recently heard: "You must be the change that you want to see in the world." Jesus, I know that with Your help, we can do anything. Together, we can make a difference for eternity and truly change the world! Mold my life and make me a reflection of You.

My one goal is that I will be a radiant light for You this year to everyone I meet and make Your name famous! Amen.

Let's start today!

"Do not conform to the pattern of this world, but be transformed by the renewing of your mind. Then you will be able to test and approve what God's will is—his good, pleasing and perfect will." Romans 12:2

WEEK 4

Joy In Believing

WEEK 4 VIDEO NOTES

Jen's Prayer -
"Lord, did I meet all Your expectations today?
Did I fulfill everything You had for me to do today?"

Philippians 3:4-8
Paul says to put no confidence in the _____.

For by grace are you saved through FAITH (Ephesians 2:8,9).

Why was Saul persecuting the church?

A Defining Moment - Acts 9:1-17
Saul meets _____ and his destiny is changed forever!
He gets a new name, a new identity, a new passion and a new purpose!

In Latin, Paul means "small" or _____.

God doesn't waste one thing that you go through.
He uses everything if you let Him!

Philippians 3:10
How can I be like Christ in His death?
What was Jesus doing when He was dying on the cross?
1. Giving _____
2. Giving the Gospel
3. Giving _____
We can do these 3 things every day!

Our citizenship is in _____ (Philippians 3:20).

"Everyone who calls on the name of the Lord will be saved" (Romans 10:13).

Joy In Believing

Jeff walked into the tallest high-rise in downtown Ft. Lauderdale located at One Financial Plaza. He was trying to get to the corner penthouse office on the top floor to see Mr. Davell, the distinguished partner of a well-known law firm. The receptionist in the lobby stopped him before he reached the guarded elevator and asked, "Excuse me, sir, do you have an appointment?"

"No ma'am, I don't."

"Well, are you here on retainer?"

"No ma'am, I'm not a paying client."

"Do you happen to be an intern here? Do you have a badge or ID or anything? I can't just let you up there to disturb Mr. Davell without some kind of qualifications," she replied politely but firmly.

"No ma'am. I'm afraid I don't have any special qualifications, but…I do have his son."

Just then a floppy-blond-haired teenager came walking around the corner and waved at the receptionist.

"I'm so sorry, Mr. Murphy. I had no idea you were with William. Please allow me to escort you to Mr. Davell's office myself."

And just like that my brother-in-law Jeff gained access not only to the penthouse office, but also to the coke machine, all the food in the break room and Mr. Davell himself.

I love how this story illustrates the wonderful, undeserved privilege that if we have the Son, we have direct access to God the Father!

In Philippians, Chapter 3, Paul issues a strong warning against anyone who would require any qualifications other than faith in Jesus Christ to gain access or a right-standing with God.

When Jesus paid for our sins on the cross, He nullified the requirements of the law. **To add any of the requirements of the law back to salvation would forfeit what Jesus accomplished on the cross. He and His true disciples taught salvation by grace and faith alone—nothing added.** Ephesians 2:8-9 says, "For it is by grace you have been saved, through faith—and this is not from yourselves, it is the gift of God—not by works, so that no one can boast."

Now at this time, salvation by means of believing in Jesus was a paradigm shift for the entire world. That's kind of the point of God putting skin on and coming into the world to walk among us—something BIG was about to happen. When Jesus came into the world, so did grace (John 1). However, the Jews had lived under the rule of the law for centuries. Similarly, the Gentiles had participated in idol worship and all types of vulgar pagan rituals trying to gain favor with their "gods." Although many of the Jews received salvation by faith in Jesus, their human tendency was to fall back into the trap of adding on some of the requirements of the law to their faith. They confused external behavior and appearance with internal spiritual maturity. Add to that the fact that Paul was commissioned to carry the gospel to the Gentiles, who the Jews referred to as "filthy dogs" because of their revolting heathen practices. Some of the Jews simply refused to accept these pagans (who just one generation ago they were forbidden to eat dinner with) into the church without making them look and act more like—well, themselves.

Take a Look: Philippians 3:1-6

No Confidence in the Flesh
Further my brothers and sisters rejoice in the Lord! It is no trouble for me to write the same things to you again, and it is a safeguard for you. ² Watch out for those dogs, those evildoers, those mutilators of the flesh. ³ For it is we who are the circumcision, we who serve God by his Spirit, who boast in Christ Jesus, and who put no confidence in the flesh— ⁴ though I myself have reasons for such confidence. If someone else thinks they have reasons to put confidence in the flesh, I have more: ⁵ circumcision the eighth day, of the people of Israel, of the tribe of Benjamin, a Hebrew of Hebrews; in regard to the law, a Pharisee; ⁶ as for zeal, persecuting the church; as for righteousness based on the law, faultless.

 Who or what does Paul say that we are to rejoice in (verse 1)?

Does he add anything else to rejoice in such as who you are, where you've come from, what you've accomplished or what you have?

Why do you think Paul calls the believers in Philippi "brothers and sisters?" Why would it have been important at this stage in church history for Paul (a distinguished Jew) to call the new European, Gentile believers by those terms?

"I will be a Father to you, and you will be my sons and daughters, says the Lord Almighty" (2 Corinthians 6:18).

It doesn't matter what race or color we are, when we accept Jesus as our Lord and Savior, we are all adopted into the same family - the family of God! We are brothers and sisters in Christ! Hallelujah!

NOTE ON "THOSE DOGS...EVILDOERS...MUTILATORS OF THE FLESH"

To emphasize his disdain for anyone teaching anything other than salvation by faith, Paul chooses the word "dogs" that the Jews typically used to refer to filthy, unbelieving Gentiles and ascribes it to the Jews who were promoting this false doctrine. Paul used a repulsive word to get their attention! There were many Jewish Christians who thought that it was necessary for the Gentiles to follow all of the Old Testament Jewish laws in order to receive salvation.

Circumcision was one of the acts of legalism these false teachers were imposing on the Gentiles. The Jewish ritual involved a "cutting around" of the flesh (Greek, peri). However, Paul uses the term for "cutting down" (Greek, kata) when he calls them "mutilators" to demonstrate that they were destroying or literally castrating the doctrine of salvation by faith. The "circumcision of the spirit" that Paul preached involved removing the sin of the heart, not the skin of the flesh. Nevertheless, it is interesting to note that Paul did require Timothy to be circumcised (Acts 16:3), not as a means of salvation, but to remove any barriers to the faith among the Jewish people for the sake of spreading the gospel. In 1 Corinthians 9:19-22, Paul explains why he and Timothy adhere to a higher standard:

Though I am free and belong to no one, I have made myself a slave to everyone, to win as many as possible. To the Jews I became like a Jew, to win the Jews. To those under the law I became like one under the law (though I myself am not under the law), so as to win those under the law. To those not having the law I became like one not having the law (though I am not free from God's law but am under Christ's law), so as to win those not having the law. To the weak I became weak, to win the weak. I have become all things to all people so that by all possible means I might save some.

🐚 *Paul gives a forceful warning with strong language. Is this the first time he has issued this warning? What is the significance of Paul repeating this warning? (verse 2)*

🐚 *What seven things does Paul list in verses 3-6 that, from a human perspective, would give him a right to have confidence in his flesh among his Jewish contemporaries? Why do you think he includes this extensive list of qualifications?*

🐚 *Do you find it shocking in verse 6 that Paul has "persecuting the church" in this list?*

Take A Look: Read Acts 9

Before Paul became a Christian, his name was Saul. Acts 9 tells the dramatic story of Saul's conversion on the road to Damascus. Once Saul met the risen Jesus, he was forever changed!

🐚 *Did God speak anything new to your heart as you read the story?*

🐚 *What did the Lord say about Saul in Acts 9:15-16?*

What was Saul going to be filled with, according to Acts 9:17?

I love this! What did Saul do immediately in Acts 9:20?

Complete Turnaround!

One of the things which fascinates me in this story is that Saul thought he was doing the right thing by persecuting Christians. He thought Christians were heretics, and he believed he was doing the work of God and protecting the Jewish faith by putting them in jail. Saul was spiritually blinded to the truth! God got his attention by a bright light that caused him to be physically blind for three days. Have you ever been blinded to the truth before? I know I have! Sometimes I think I'm heading in the right direction; then God stops me in my tracks and shows me He has a very different plan for me.

Has that ever happened to you before where you were going in one direction and God completely changed your destiny?

If we are honest with ourselves, most of us question the existence of God at some point in our lives. Perhaps it's just a small nagging doubt—Is God really real? Yes! He is so real! How else can you explain this story! Saul, who had the authority to persecute those who believed in Jesus, suddenly makes a 180-degree turn. He becomes the one who suffers and eventually dies for his faith in Jesus. Paul was hand-picked by Jesus to become the greatest missionary. He was headed in the wrong direction, and God reached down and gave him a new destiny!

Saul is completely transformed from "Saul the Persecutor" to "Paul the Preacher." If God could turn Saul's life around, think about what God could do in your life once your heart is completely surrendered to Him.

I grew up thinking God changed Saul's name to Paul, but the Bible never says that God changed his name. Most likely, Saul chose to be called Paul because it would have been a more common name among the Gentiles, and his new calling in life was to be a missionary to the Gentiles. He had a new name, a new passion and a new identity!

When we accept Christ as our Lord and Savior, we too receive a new identity—the old things are passed away and all things become new (2 Corinthians 5:17)!

Let's Get Real:

🐚 *In what ways do you "put confidence in the flesh?"*

🐚 *Take a moment to ask God to reveal to you some areas where you are trusting in the flesh more than trusting in Him. Wait on Him in prayer and then confess those areas out loud or in writing before Him.*

🐚 *What kind of people are the most difficult for you to accept or extend grace to? Is there anyone like that in your church, neighborhood or sphere of influence? Ask God to show you one simple act of kindness you could do for that person. Keep in mind that God's Word says, "kindness leads to repentance" (Romans 2:4).*

NOTE ON "OF THE TRIBE OF BENJAMIN"

Paul boasted that he could trace his family origin to the tribe of Benjamin, the favored tribe of King Saul, Israel's first king. No doubt Paul was originally named after King Saul before he changed his name from Saul to Paul. Benjamin was also the tribe blessed by Moses as "the beloved of the LORD… whom the LORD loves [and who] rests between his shoulders" (Deuteronomy 33:12), in whose territory sat the Holy City of Jerusalem itself. They were also notable because they alone had joined Judah in loyalty to the Davidic covenant when the Kingdom of Israel split after Solomon's death.

NOTE ON THE DOCTRINE OF SALVATION: JUSTIFICATION, SANCTIFICATION, GLORIFICATION

For centuries, Bible scholars have explained the miracle of salvation in three parts: Justification (the point that you believe and receive Christ's righteousness just as if you've never sinned), Sanctification (the process of growing and maturing to become more like Christ as evidence that He is alive in you), and Glorification (the future event when you will be united with Christ in Heaven and given a new body and clothed in righteousness forever). In this passage, Paul makes reference to all three of these parts of salvation:

Justification – "found in [Christ], not having a righteousness of my own" (verse 9).

Sanctification – "I want to know Christ…not that I have already obtained all of this…" (verses 10-12).

Glorification – "for which God has called me heavenward in Christ Jesus" (verse 14).

Take a Look: Philippians 3:7-11

Everything Without Jesus = Nothing

⁷ But whatever were gains to me I now consider loss for the sake of Christ. ⁸ What is more, I consider everything a loss because of the surpassing worth of knowing Christ Jesus my Lord, for whose sake I have lost all things. I consider them garbage, that I may gain Christ ⁹ and be found in him, not having a righteousness of my own that comes from the law, but that which is through faith in Christ—the righteousness that comes from God on the basis of faith. ¹⁰ I want to know Christ—yes, to know the power of his resurrection and participation in his sufferings, becoming like him in his death, ¹¹ and so, somehow, attaining to the resurrection from the dead.

How would you summarize verses 7-9? Write the message of these verses in your own words. Why is this message so important? How could this message increase our joy?

How does Paul describe righteous acts in verse 8? Does this make you feel relieved or uncomfortable?

🐚 *What are the first 5 words of verse 10? According to Paul, what does "knowing Christ" involve?*

🐚 *What does Paul imply will enable you to know the power of the resurrection? Does it have anything to do with your own righteousness?*

NOTE "GARBAGE"

The word Paul uses to describe his own righteous acts is a graphic term (Greek, skubala) that is sometimes translated as "dung" or "food leftovers" that get thrown to the dogs. In either case, it is something disgusting that gets discarded as waste. This coincides with the prophet Isaiah's teaching in the Old Testament: "All of us have become like one who is unclean, and all our righteous acts are like filthy rags" (Isaiah 64:6).

Take a Look: Philippians 3:12-14

Press Toward the Goal

¹² Not that I have already obtained all this, or have already arrived at my goal, but I press on to take hold of that for which Christ Jesus took hold of me. ¹³ Brothers and sisters, I do not consider myself yet to have taken hold of it. But one thing I do: Forgetting what is behind and straining toward what is ahead, ¹⁴ I press on toward the goal to win the prize for which God has called me heavenward in Christ Jesus.

Circle the verbs that stand out to you in the verses above.

Eyes on the Goal

Having a daughter with a brain injury made me a nervous wreck watching my son Josh play varsity football as a ninth grader—especially when his helmet would fly off during a tackle. We already had one brain injury in our family, and we surely didn't need another one! Josh loved playing defense, which meant he was usually tackling guys twice his size. I would be praying out loud in the stands as Josh was literally at the bottom of the pile on almost every defensive play. I know the other parents probably thought I was crazy, but I didn't care because that was my little boy out there.

One game that I will never forget is when Josh got an interception and was running for a "pick 6" while the entire opposing team was pursuing him. The crowd went wild, and I was screaming at the top of my lungs as Josh scored a touchdown! After the game, I hugged Josh and said, "Your interception was amazing! I'm so proud of you! But weren't you afraid of the 11 guys that were chasing you?" Josh laughed at me and said, **"Mom, you can't play the game looking over your shoulder. You have to keep your eyes on the goal."**

That's what I picture when I read Philippians 3:13-14— Josh running toward the end zone and never looking back. We all have to do that in life. God tells us to keep pushing forward towards the goal and trust Him for the next step. We can't let our past failures paralyze us and keep us out of the game. Just like Paul we have to say, "I press on toward the goal to win the prize for which God has called me."

ACTION STEP

WRITE DOWN ONE THING YOU HAVE LOST OR GIVEN UP BECAUSE OF CHRIST AND HIS CALLING ON YOUR LIFE. FIND A PLACE TO DIG A HOLE, BURY IT AND DON'T LOOK BACK!

Let's Get Real

Your greatest calling usually comes out of your greatest crisis. Your passion comes from your pain. What has your calling cost you? Are you mourning your loss or celebrating it?

How does "forgetting the past" fit with Paul's teaching on salvation through faith alone? Does his teaching give you joy?

Are you really believing or buying Paul's message? If you are still hanging on to your past, what might you be implying about Jesus and His gift of salvation?

🐚   *Name one thing you need to forget from your past (a failure, mistake, desire or success) that is keeping you from reaching for future success.*

🐚   *Name one reason you think Christ took hold of your heart? What is it that He is calling you to take hold of? Are you moving towards or away from that goal?*

Take a Look: Philippians 3:15-21

Citizens of Heaven

[15] *All of us, then, who are mature should take such a view of things. And if on some point you think differently, that too God will make clear to you.* [16] *Only let us live up to what we have already attained.* [17] *Join together in following my example, brothers and sisters, and just as you have us as a model, keep your eyes on those who live as we do.* [18] *For, as I have often told you before and now tell you again even with tears, many live as enemies of the cross of Christ.* [19] *Their destiny is destruction, their god is their stomach, and their glory is in their shame. Their mind is set on earthly things.* [20] *But our citizenship is in heaven. And we eagerly await a Savior from there, the Lord Jesus Christ,* [21] *who, by the power that enables him to bring everything under his control, will transform our lowly bodies so that they will be like his glorious body.*

🐚   *According to verses 15-16, what is the best way to deal with someone you disagree with?*

🐚   *In verse 17, what does Paul urge Christians to do? Why are spiritual role models important? What could the dangers of spiritual role models be?*

What is the cause of Paul's tears? How does Paul describe the "enemies of the cross?"

What does Paul mean by "their god is their belly?"

Instead of living a crucified life to serve God and others, "enemies of the cross" live to gratify their own physical desires and passions. They live for pleasure and indulge themselves. They pursue material possessions instead of living a life that will count for eternity. There are those who profess Christ but are spiritual counterfeits. They are walking in the flesh, instead of in the Spirit.

What will happen to the mind governed by the flesh, according to Romans 8:5-8?

What does 2 Timothy 3:1-5 say will happen in the last days?

🐚 *Where was Paul's true citizenship?*

🐚 *What was Paul looking forward to in verses 20-21? How might his confidence in these beliefs enable him to face suffering with joy?*

Let's Get Real

🐚 *What makes you most excited about heaven? What is the first thing you want to do when you get there? What aspect of having a new, "glorious" body will you be most grateful for?*

🐚 *In what ways do you live like you are a "citizen of heaven?" How do you feel when you focus on heaven?*

NOTE ON "OUR CITIZENSHIP IS IN HEAVEN"

The residents of Philippi were technically citizens of Rome. They lived in a Roman colony within the region of Macedonia. Even though they were far away from Rome, they were still Romans. Likewise, Christians make up a colony of heaven on earth. Even though they are far away physically from the location of heaven, they still belong in heaven. The verb Paul uses for "is" (Greek, huparchei) indicates that this citizenship in heaven is a present possession. It is the same verb used to describe Jesus "being" in the form of God (Philippians 2:6). Just as the deity of Christ can never be taken away, the Christian's citizenship in heaven can never be taken away. Hallelujah—praise the Lord!

🐚 *In what ways do you live more like a citizen of earth with your "mind set on earthly things?" How do you feel when you focus on earthly things?*

Mirror Mirror

Lately when I look in the mirror, I'm not sure who that woman is looking back at me! She sure doesn't look the way she looks in my head. She has stretch marks from giving birth to 10-pound babies, a scar across her forehead and a tan that looks more like dark spots.

Recently, I was pretty proud of myself because I went on a strict diet, did strenuous weight training and lost 20 pounds. Now that's quite an accomplishment for a girl who has more ice cream than coffee in her morning cup and a nightly routine of chips and sour cream before bed. I was actually starting to feel better about myself, until I was speaking at a church where I played a video of our story. After the service, a woman came up to me and said, "You've lost a lot of weight! I didn't think you were the same girl in the video, but then I saw the big mole on your face and I knew it was you!" HaHa!

So much for confidence in the flesh! To top it off, she continued, "How much weight have you lost anyway?"

I said, "Around 20 pounds."

She shook her head and said, "Oh no, you had to have lost at least 50 or 60!" I wasn't sure if I should laugh or cry!

I embrace aging and scars and stretch marks because they all make me look forward to Heaven! I can't wait to have a new body there, and I can't wait to see Jesus face to face!

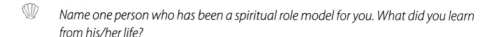 *Name one person who has been a spiritual role model for you. What did you learn from his/her life?*

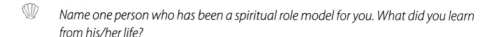 *If you have never had a spiritual role model, pray and ask God to send you one.*

Also, be looking for someone younger in their faith that you could mentor and encourage.

Grammy Jean

One of my greatest spiritual role models was my Grammy Jean. She was always happy and laughing. She passed away at 92 in a nursing home near my house, where I was able to spend many precious moments with her the past few years. She loved Jesus with all of her heart! She kept a ring of handwritten Bible verses next to her bed. Many times I would pop in to see her and Grammy Jean would be working on memorizing those verses—at 92. She loved God's word and quoted it out loud daily! In fact, even when she started to show signs of dementia, she could still quote hundreds of verses! My other favorite memory of Grammy Jean is that she was always singing. The last video recording we have of her was with my cousin Heidi singing "Jesus Is the Sweetest Name I Know." These were her last spoken words:

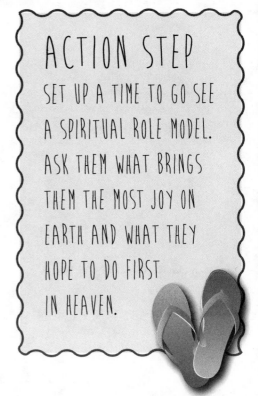

ACTION STEP
SET UP A TIME TO GO SEE A SPIRITUAL ROLE MODEL. ASK THEM WHAT BRINGS THEM THE MOST JOY ON EARTH AND WHAT THEY HOPE TO DO FIRST IN HEAVEN.

> *Jesus is the sweetest name I know,*
> *And He's just the same as His lovely name,*
> *And that's the reason why I love Him so;*
> *Oh, Jesus is the sweetest name I know.*

At the end of life Jesus is all you need.

Jesus + Nothing = Everything!

Life is not about what you've done, but what He did for you on the cross!

JOURNAL RESPONSE

(Take a moment to reflect on Who God is and write a response to Him).

God, thank You for the way You… Thank You for the time You…

God, You are so…

God, forgive me for…

God, help me to …

God, I will trust You to…

PRAYER FROM JEN

When I Need Faith!

Dear Everlasting Father,

As I go through this day, I want to experience You. Lord, please give me faith. You promise in Scripture that if I have faith the size of a mustard seed, I can move mountains in my life. Nothing is too big for You! I love the verse that says, "I believe, help my unbelief." Father, give me faith to believe and trust You for the big and small mountains. Without faith it is impossible to please You. I know that You delight when I pray BIG! Bold prayers honor You. Amen.

Waiting in expectation…

"Immediately the boy's father exclaimed, 'I do believe; help me overcome my unbelief!'" Mark 9:24

WEEK 5

Joy In
Giving

WEEK 5 VIDEO NOTES

God made us for relationship.

Cure for Anxiety = Pray About Everything With Thanksgiving (Philippians 4:6-7)

What is God's will for me (I Thessalonians 5:16-18)?

1. _____ always

2. _____ continually

3. Give _____ in ALL circumstances.

Checklist:

Is it _____, noble, right, lovely, _____, admirable

(Philippians 4:8)?

What you put into your heart and mind will come out (Luke 6:45).

… the mouth speaks what the heart is full of.

Secret of Contentment = _____ (Philippians 4:11-13)

As you are giving, God promises to meet your every need (Luke 6:38).

Needs can be financial, emotional, social, and spiritual.

Jehovah Jireh - God is my PROVIDER!

Christ lives IN you - Hope lives in you (Colossians 1:27)!

What is one thing you can do today to become more like Jesus?
Take a minute and write a prayer of commitment to God.

_____

_____

_____

_____

Joy In Giving

Andy and I were married seven years before we bought our first "real" house. I was so excited to finally decorate my very own home and buy new furniture. I had dreamed for years about all the things I would buy when the time came, particularly my bedroom suite. I had seen a gorgeous cherry Victorian bedroom set complete with marble accents and crystal knobs at a bed and breakfast and tucked away the manufacturer's information for the perfect timing. I had my heart set on it. I could just envision how beautiful it would look in my new bedroom. I contacted the seller and was a little shocked that this particular set would exhaust most of my furniture budget for the entire house, but it didn't matter; I had waited a long time and thought I deserved to splurge. After all, Andy and I were still sleeping on the same bed I had since I was in middle school.

The day it arrived, I sat on the bed relishing my new armoire. Looking at the reflection of the bed in the mirror, the thought occurred to me that this set would look a lot better if I had silk bedding to go with it. Too bad I had already blown my budget. Then I noticed the dresser didn't quite fill up the wall like I had expected. Wait a minute…this was supposed to be the day my dream came true; but somehow, it was just a little disappointing. I thought I would feel happy but instead I found myself suffering from what my husband calls post-purchase dissidence.

About this same time, a sweet family we knew was struggling financially. We anonymously gave them some money for groceries. I remember thinking - *oh, if I hadn't spent so much on that bedroom set, we could have given a lot more.*

A move or two later, the mirror was cracked and some of the crystal handles were missing. I learned one of life's most valuable lessons from that Victorian bedroom suite—stuff doesn't satisfy your soul. I had found much more joy in giving grocery money to a family in need than indulging on my dream furniture. Jesus knew what He was talking about when He said, "It's more blessed to give than to receive."

Paul ends the book of Philippians with a discussion on giving and the joy it produces for both the giver and the recipient. Before he begins this discussion, however, he tackles some heart issues. I believe that is because giving is a matter of the heart. Jesus also said, "Wherever your treasure is, there the desires of your heart will be also" (Matthew 6:21, NLT).

God doesn't lead us to give so He can have more of our stuff. **God leads us to give and give up so He can have more of our hearts. The more God has of our hearts, the greater our joy.** Now don't get me wrong—God isn't upset when we buy new furniture or acquire nice things. His word says that He "gives us everything for our enjoyment" (1 Timothy 6:17). But…there is a big difference between enjoyment and joy. Enjoyment is temporary. Joy is lasting. True joy comes from giving up the fleeting for the eternal. And that, dear friends, requires some work in our hearts.

Take a Look: Philippians 4:1-3

Live in Unity

Therefore, my brothers and sisters, you whom I love and long for, my joy and crown, stand firm in the Lord in this way, dear friends! ² I plead with Euodia and I plead with Syntyche to be of the same mind in the Lord. ³ Yes, and I ask you, my true companion, help these women since they have contended at my side in the cause of the gospel, along with Clement and the rest of my co-workers, whose names are in the book of life.

According to verse 1, who or what gave Paul joy?

What words or phrases does Paul choose in these verses to describe the people in the church of Philippi? Based on your study of Philippians so far, what are some things Paul had "given up" for the church? Does he seem to have any regrets?

What problem in the church of Philippi did Paul address (verse 2)?

I like how Philippians 4:2 in the NLT version says, "Please, because you belong to the Lord, settle your disagreement."

What reasons did Paul give for these women to lay aside their differences?

In whom did he ask them to stand firm (verse 1)?

NOTE ON EUODIA AND SYNTYCHE

How would you like to be remembered for arguing? Both Euodia and Syntyche had served alongside Paul and had their names written in the Lamb's Book of Life, but they are called out by name for causing disunity in the church. Evidently, the problem had escalated enough that Paul chose to address it publicly. Or perhaps, addressing it publicly is Paul's way of reminding everyone that disunity between a few members directly affects the entire body, as well as hindering outsiders from becoming insiders. Paul reminds these ladies that they will spend eternity together in Heaven so they might as well work out their differences on earth. In an effort to keep them from ruining the evangelistic outreach of the church, Paul pleads with them to return to "one mind in the Lord." Paul also pleads with his "true companion" (perhaps Lydia) to "help these women" reconcile their differences as a mediator, establishing an example for church discipline and intervention in the arena of unity.

Let's Get Real

Who or what gives you the most joy?

Do you invest more time and resources in the things or people you just mentioned above or in something else? Why or why not?

I have heard it said that the only thing you get to take to Heaven is people. Who will be in heaven someday because of your influence or resources?

Have you ever had a disagreement with another believer? How did it end?

When you consider the fact that all believers will spend an eternity in Heaven together, how should we handle our disagreements with other believers?

🐚 *If we are "standing firm in the Lord" do we need to stand firm in order to work out our disagreements with other believers?*

🐚 *What things or people have you allowed to rob your joy?*

🐚 *Do you have any rights or things that you feel entitled to that God is urging you to give up for the sake of His church or His people?*

Write Out: Philippians 4:4-7

Cure for Anxiety

_____

_____

_____

_____

_____

_____

Those four verses that you just wrote are probably the most quotable verses of the entire book of Philippians. They are very straightforward. They contain four imperative commands (FYI—These are not optional) with one big important truth sandwiched in the middle, followed by a very helpful hint at the end. See if you can pick out the four commands, the truth in the middle, and the hint at the end…

ACTION STEP

PRAY THIS SIMPLE PRAYER: GOD, WHAT DO YOU WANT ME TO GIVE UP FOR YOU AND YOUR PEOPLE TODAY? IS THERE AN ARGUMENT OR A PERSONAL RIGHT THAT I AM HOLDING ON TO THAT IS HINDERING YOUR WORK? IS THERE A RESOURCE OR A GIFT YOU HAVE BLESSED ME WITH THAT COULD ADVANCE YOUR WORK IF I LET IT GO?

The PEACE Formula

Command #1:

_____

Command #2:

_____

Truth:

_____

Command #3:

_____

Command #4:

_____

Hint:

_____

Big End Result =

_____

(P.S. The answers are included on the pages to follow)

Command #1 – Rejoice Always

Evidently, rejoicing is so essential to spiritual maturity that God commands it twice! Plus, he requires it always! It's not easy to rejoice always. Try thinking of the command to rejoice as "re-joy." **God is not asking us to summon up joy from our own strength; He is simply asking us to reflect the joy He gives us that already exists abundantly in Him.** He says, "Rejoice in the Lord," not in your circumstances. We simply re-joy or re-gift the joy that exists in Him and His nature. Remember, He is the source; we are just a reflection of His image.

Have you ever re-gifted something? How does the concept of "re-joy" or being a "reflection of God's joy" help us to have joy in all of our circumstances? Does God's nature change with circumstances? Then neither should His reflection—ouch!

Command #2 – Be Gentle

The word "gentleness" (Greek, epiekes) can also be translated "forbearing spirit." A person with a "forbearing spirit" bears trouble calmly, is not revengeful, does not seek to retaliate, embraces patience and goodwill, and rejects the temptation to project their hurt on others. Gentleness does not mean weakness. On the contrary, gentleness is evidence of supernatural strength at work. **A "forbearing spirit" means we are "bearing" trouble as if it is "for" our own good.** Is that not what we are called to do as fellow-sufferers and slaves of Christ?

 What are the benefits of being gentle? Can you think of any examples in Scripture where being gentle ("forbearing spirit") required great strength? What were the end results of being gentle?

Truth in the Middle: "The Lord is Near."

Let's be real. These four commands are not easy. In fact, they are quite impossible apart from Christ. Jesus said, "Apart from Me, you can do nothing" (John 15:5). But He also said, "I am with you always, even unto the end of the world" (Matthew 28:20). The word "near" (Greek, eggus) refers to both time and space, meaning this truth refers both to the imminence of Christ's return as well as His omnipresence and presence within the believer. There is no physical space or place where God is not present. And with every ticking second, we draw closer to the time when He will return and establish His Kingdom on earth. **God's presence is a reality, period! We just have to awaken to the awareness that He is always at hand.**

 What helps you to be alert to God's presence? What hinders your awareness of God's presence? How could you begin each day with an awareness that God is near?

Command #3 – Don't Worry About Anything

Anxiety is caused by uncertainty. When we realize the One who knows our future is near, we have nothing to fear. It's like taking a test with the answer key—you can't mess it up. You may not be able to see or even understand all of the answers, but the solutions to all of your problems are right within you in the Person of the Holy Spirit.

What do you worry most about? Write out your top three worries here:

1.   2.   3.

Command #4 – Pray About Everything

Prayer is the antidote to worry.

Take a moment to write a prayer about your three biggest worries:

_____

_____

_____

_____

Helpful Hint: "With Thanksgiving"

These two words are essential. They remove the human barriers of anxiety and selfish ambition by ushering us into the throne room of God. Thanksgiving makes the central truth "the Lord is near" a reality. Psalms instructs us to "enter his gates with thanksgiving" and "come into His courts with praise" (Psalm 100:4). **The quickest route to coming face to face with God is *through thanksgiving*. The difference between praying and whining is *with thanksgiving*. The difference between what we want and what God desires is *with thanksgiving*. The difference between praying in our power and praying through God's power is *with thanksgiving*!**

Now, let's rewrite our prayers that we wrote above with thanksgiving this time. See the difference?

_____

_____

_____

_____

Praise Him in Advance

Often when we are driving to speak at an event, Jen will pray out loud in the car. She will start praising God in advance for all the people who are going to get saved and all the lives that are going to be changed. She is expecting God to show up! Sometimes she starts giggling and says "God is speaking to my heart and it's going to be big! He is going to do a mighty work today!" I can't tell you how much this encourages me because usually I am worried about all the details and often Jen is struggling and doesn't feel good. I have learned by watching Jen that there is a huge difference between begging God to show up and thanking Him in advance as if it has already happened! When we praise God, He fills our hearts with peace and puts our focus on who He is instead of our circumstances. When we have that kind of faith, there is no limit to what God can do!

The Big End Result = Peace

Paul says that when we 1. Rejoice always, 2. Be gentle, 3. Stop worrying, and 4. Start praying *with thanksgiving*, the end result is peace—an unexplainable peace that guards our hearts and minds in Christ Jesus. It's funny to think of "peace" as a weapon. When I think of "guards," I think of guns, tanks, swords and the threat of battle breaking out at any moment—the last thing I think of is peace. The word "guard" comes from a Greek verb (horao), which means "to see before or look out." It's a military term referring to soldiers who were placed on duty to protect, like the soldiers assigned to guard Paul in prison. **God's peace sees trouble before it comes; it prepares our hearts and minds in advance.** It's truly beyond human explanation; you have to experience it, and God has promised it to you in 1 Corinthians 2:9:

"No eye has seen, no ear has heard, no mind has conceived what God has prepared [in advance] for those who love Him."

 Tell about a time that you have experienced the "peace of God that passes understanding."

PRAYER FROM JEN

When I Need Peace

My Lord, My Security is in You!

I need Your perfect peace today. I am reminded of the story of Jesus and His disciples who were on the Sea of Galilee... and a huge storm came. Jesus was asleep in the bottom of the boat, and the disciples woke him up in a panic saying, "Master, don't you care? Our lives are in danger!" Jesus stood up and stretched out his hands and said, "Peace, be still!" Immediately, the storm stopped and the disciples said, "Who is this, that even the wind and the waves obey Him?" In my life, when the storm is raging all around me, help me to picture You standing up in the midst of my circumstances, saying, "Peace, be still!" Amen.

You are more than enough!

"Peace I leave with you; my peace I give you. I do not give to you as the world gives. Do not let your hearts be troubled and do not be afraid." John 14:27

Take a Look: Philippians 4:8-13

Aligning Our Thoughts with the God of Peace

⁸ *Finally, brothers and sisters, whatever is true, whatever is noble, whatever is right, whatever is pure, whatever is lovely, whatever is admirable—if anything is excellent or praiseworthy—think about such things. ⁹ Whatever you have learned or received or heard from me, or seen in me—put it into practice. And the God of peace will be with you.¹⁰ I rejoiced greatly in the Lord that at last you renewed your concern for me. Indeed, you were concerned, but you had no opportunity to show it. ¹¹ I am not saying this because I am in need, for I have learned to be content whatever the circumstances. ¹² I know what it is to be in need, and I know what it is to have plenty. I have learned the secret of being content in any and every situation, whether well fed or hungry, whether living in plenty or in want. ¹³ I can do all this through him who gives me strength.*

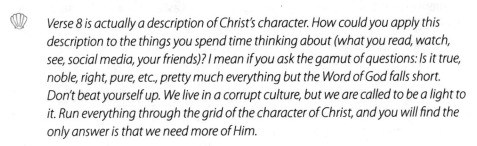 *Verse 8 is actually a description of Christ's character. How could you apply this description to the things you spend time thinking about (what you read, watch, see, social media, your friends)? I mean if you ask the gamut of questions: Is it true, noble, right, pure, etc., pretty much everything but the Word of God falls short. Don't beat yourself up. We live in a corrupt culture, but we are called to be a light to it. Run everything through the grid of the character of Christ, and you will find the only answer is that we need more of Him.*

How can you implement more of God's Word into your routine? ***What could you give up for the next seven days to fit more of Christ in?***

(Verse 9) Can you imagine saying to your biological children or children in the faith, "Whatever you have heard from me or seen in me, put into practice"? What qualities do you hope your kids or loved ones never learn from watching you? Ask God to cover those gaps today.

A Mom's Prayer

I know a pastor's wife I respect wholeheartedly who raised four amazing kids, in spite of serving in several churches plagued with disagreements and division. My friend and her husband have literally and sadly "been through hell" in the church, and yet, all four of her children are still faithfully serving in churches today. I asked her what her secret was, and she said, "I have always prayed that my children would never hold the sin they witnessed in the church against Jesus." I love that prayer! I would add that I pray, "Lord Jesus, help my children to never hold the sin they see in their parents against you!"

 In verse 11, Paul says, "I have learned to be content in any situation." Is contentment our natural human reaction? Why do you think Paul said he had to "learn" it? What is the secret to contentment according to verse 13?

Let's Get Real

 What is the one thing that stirs discontentment in you more than anything else?

Think about your abilities, your possessions, your relationship status and your career. What is the one thing you would change if you could?

 What if this was where God has the greatest potential to do the greatest work in your life? What if this was how you came to know the mystery of the joy and power of God in your life?

Contentment does not mean being self-sufficient; it means being God-sufficient. Paul wrote, "My [God's] grace is sufficient for you, for my power is made perfect in weakness. Therefore I will boast all the more gladly about my weaknesses, so that Christ's power may rest on me" (2 Corinthians 2:9). Spend a moment bragging about your weaknesses (those areas of discontentment) and thank God that you get to know more of Him through your weakness.

Joy in Giving and Receiving

If you've ever had to depend on someone else for your livelihood, you know what it's like to ask for help. It can be truly humbling. My friend Vicki had worked a prominent, successful job when God called her to leave her comfort zone and serve in a non-profit organization that required her to raise her full salary by faith. After providing for herself for many years, it was a little embarrassing to ask others for support. She was worried that friends and family members would think she was lazy, or at least crazy. In fact, she was certain several of her friends started avoiding her like the plague for fear she would ask them for money. Then she met Mark and Judy. Even though Mark and Judy didn't have much to spare in the area of finances, they had a sacrificial heart. When Vicki approached Mark and Judy and timidly asked for their support and prayers, she was blown away by their response. They wrote the kindest note that said: *"Thank you so much for thinking of us. It is such an honor that you would count us worthy to help make a difference in people's lives. We would have missed out on a tremendous blessing if you had not included us."* Then Mark and Judy "put their money where their mouth was" and gave a very sacrificial gift beyond their means or ability. Not only did Vicki save the note, she told me later that Mark and Judy's response was the tipping point for her in living by faith. Because of their excitement to give, Vicki began to view giving as a blessing and not a duty. She was no longer embarrassed to ask people to join her vision with boldness and the assurance that God was not just using her but the people who would support her as well.

The amazing part of the story is that a few months later, Mark and Judy were cleaning out their basement and found a wad of cash more than double the amount they had sacrificed to give to Vicki. They had forgotten that they had stored some money away before Y2K in case of a crisis, and God helped them find it right after they had given to my friend Vicki.

Take a Look: Philippians 4:14-19

As You Are Giving, God Will Provide!

¹⁴ Yet it was good of you to share in my troubles. ¹⁵ Moreover, as you Philippians know, in the early days of your acquaintance with the gospel, when I set out from Macedonia, not one church shared with me in the matter of giving and receiving, except you only; ¹⁶ for even when I was in Thessalonica, you sent me aid more than once when I was in need. ¹⁷ Not that I desire your gifts; what I desire is that more be credited to your account. ¹⁸ I have received full payment and have more than enough. I am amply supplied, now that I have received from Epaphroditus the gifts you sent. They are a fragrant offering, an acceptable sacrifice, pleasing to God. ¹⁹ And my God will meet all your needs according to the riches of his glory in Christ Jesus.

What did Paul say about the Philippian church sharing with him during his troubles (verse 14)?

How often had the Philippian church given financial gifts to Paul (verse 16-18)? What does this indicate that God must have done for the Philippian Christians in order for them to continue to give over and over (see 2 Corinthians 9:10-11)?

What did Paul desire for the Philippian Christians (verse 17)? Did his desires have to do with their stuff or their hearts?

How did Paul, the receiver, describe the gifts the Philippians sent to him (verse 18)? Who were they pleasing when they gave to Paul?

🐚 *What does verse 19 indicate about their giving? When you give sacrificially, whose riches are you relying on?*

Jehovah-Jireh is one of my favorite names for God. It means "The Lord Will Provide." Abraham first used this name for God in Genesis 22:14 when God provided a ram to be sacrificed in place of Isaac. There have been many times in my life when I have cried out to God as my Jehovah-Jireh and asked Him to come to my rescue and meet my needs.

Let's Get Real

🐚 *If giving enables you to rely on God's riches instead of your own, how might sacrificial giving result in joy rather than stress? How could a pattern of regular giving change the way you view your finances?*

🐚 *When have you given to refresh others and been replenished and refreshed by God?*

🐚 *What are you doing right now to show God that you want to advance His Kingdom and rely on His riches? Is your giving producing joy in your life and in the lives of others? Is your giving a pleasing sacrifice to God, or just your leftovers?*

🐚 *Think About It: How much would you have to give to be relying on God's riches and not your own riches?*

Take a Look: Philippians 4:20-23

Farewell Blessing

[20] To our God and Father be glory for ever and ever. Amen.
[21] Greet all God's people in Christ Jesus. The brothers and sisters who are with me send greetings. [22] All God's people here send you greetings, especially those who belong to Caesar's household. [23] The grace of the Lord Jesus Christ be with your spirit. Amen.

According to verse 20, what is the overall purpose of Paul's ministry and letter?

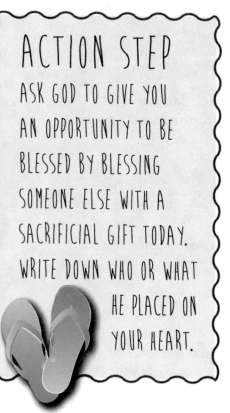

ACTION STEP

ASK GOD TO GIVE YOU AN OPPORTUNITY TO BE BLESSED BY BLESSING SOMEONE ELSE WITH A SACRIFICIAL GIFT TODAY. WRITE DOWN WHO OR WHAT HE PLACED ON YOUR HEART.

What is significant about the phrase "all God's people," considering the historical time frame of this letter?

What do you think verse 23 means? Why is this an appropriate ending for a letter about choosing joy?

Let's Get Real

What can you learn from Paul's parting words? What thoughts do you tend to leave others with when you depart from their presence?

🐚 *What is your biggest takeaway from the book of Philippians?*

🐚 *What is your favorite verse in Philippians and why?*

🐚 *Write down at least one way God's Word has changed your life over the past few weeks.*

Personal Note from Linda

The most life-changing thing that God spoke to my heart through this study was that joy is a gift from God. There are many days when I try so hard to choose joy and work hard at having joy and I still fail miserably. God was whispering in my ear as I was studying Philippians, "Linda stop trying so hard and just be a reflection of Me. If you don't have joy, you simply need to spend more time in My Presence. The more time you spend with Me, the more joy you will have. I give you joy as a gift so you can re-gift it to others. It's not something you have to work at or do. It is my free gift to you."
What a priceless treasure! The gift of JOY!

JOURNAL RESPONSE

(Take a moment to reflect on Who God is and write a response to Him).

God, thank You for the way You… Thank You for the time You…

God, You are so…

God, forgive me for…

God, help me to …

God, I will trust You to…

PRAYER FROM JEN

When I Need to Dream Again!

Dear Purpose-Giver,

Please give me the ability to dream again. I want to experience You. I don't want to limit Your power in and through my life. Please use me to my fullest potential. Help me to rise above my circumstances. I know I can do all things through Christ who strengthens me. Thank you for making a way when there seems to be no way. Give me Your vision Lord! Thank you for speaking to my heart that You aren't done with me yet. The best is yet to come, and it will far exceed anything I've ever dreamed or imagined possible. Amen.

Praising You in advance!

"Take delight in the Lord, and he will give you the desires of your heart."
Psalm 37:4

Selected Bibliography:

Briscoe, Stuart. *Happiness Beyond Our Happenings*. Wheaton, Illinois: Harold Shaw Publishers, 1993.

Caird, G.B. *Paul's Letters from Prison (Ephesians, Philippians, Colossians, Philemon)*. Oxford: Oxford University Press, 1976.

Dobson, Ed & Edward Hindson. *The Knowing Jesus Study Bible*. Grand Rapids: Zondervan, 1999.

George, Elizabeth. *Philippians: Experiencing God's Peace*. Eugene, Oregon: Harvest House Publishers, 2000.

Gromacki, Robert. *Philippians & Colossians: Joy and Completeness in Christ.* Chattanooga: AMG Publishers, 2003.

Hendricksen, William. *New Testament Commentary: The Epistle of Paul to the Philippians*. Grand Rapids: Baker Book House, 1975.

O'Brian, Peter T. *The Epistle to the Philippians: A Commentary on the Greek Text.* Grand Rapids: Eerdmans, 1991.

Theilman, Frank. *The NIV Application Commentary: Philippians.* Grand Rapids: Zondervan, 1995.

NOTES

NOTES

NOTES

OTHER RESOURCES BY LINDA BARRICK AND HOPE OUT LOUD

Available at www.hopeoutloud.com

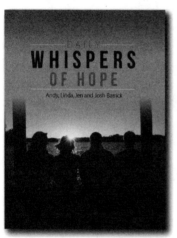

Daily Whispers of Hope

Join Andy, Linda, Jen and Josh on a journey of courage and faith in *Daily Whispers of Hope*. These 70 Scripture-based devotions are complete with reflection questions, promises from God's Word and guided prayers for quiet moments alone with the Savior. This book is for everyone! Through the pages of this book, God will whisper hope and encouragement to your heart.

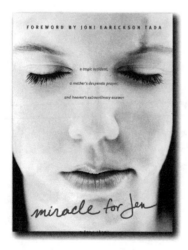

Miracle for Jen

One minute can change your whole life. The Barrick family's life was irrevocably changed when a drunk driver careened into their van at eighty miles an hour. The entire family was hurt—but fifteen-year-old Jennifer's injuries were so devastating that paramedics thought she had no chance to live. Discover, through this story of unfolding miracles and deep lessons about forgiveness, how God turned normal into extraordinary.

Miracle for Jen is also available at Amazon.com

Hope Out Loud Prayers

Jen now has what we will have in heaven some day: an intimate, uninhibited, communication with the Lord of Lords! In this prayer book are some of her personal *Hope Out Loud Prayers* that will minister to your heart and soul.

Jen's prayers are personal reflections of her relationship with God and reflect such things as:

When I Have Lost Hope
When I'm Doubting - Is God Real?
When I Don't Want To Forgive
When I Am Afraid
When I Need Joy

"This book is for everyone who is hurting. I still hurt and struggle every day, but I am clinging to the promises of God's Word. When I pray out loud, God fills me with His strength and courage. He whispers hope in my ear…" - Jen

**To order, please go to Hopeoutloud.com
or email Andy@Hopeoutloud.com**

www.hopeoutloud.com